Hockey

ANATOMY

Hockey

ANATOMY

Michael Terry, M.D.

Paul Goodman

HUMAN KINETICS

Library of Congress Cataloging-in-Publication Data

Names: Terry, Michael, 1971- | Goodman, Paul, 1974-
Title: Hockey anatomy / Michael Terry, Paul Goodman.
Description: Champaign, IL : Human Kinetics, [2019]
Identifiers: LCCN 2018012594 (print) | LCCN 2017044916 (ebook) | ISBN
9781492566465 (ebook) | ISBN 9781492535881 (print)
Subjects: LCSH: Hockey--Training. | Hockey--Physiological aspects.
Classification: LCC GV848.3 (print) | LCC GV848.3 .T47 2019 (ebook) | DDC
796.356--dc23
LC record available at https://lccn.loc.gov/2018012594

ISBN: 978-1-4925-3588-1 (print)

This publication is written and published to provide accurate and authoritative information relevant to the subject matter presented. It is published and sold with the understanding that the author and publisher are not engaged in rendering legal, medical, or other professional services by reason of their authorship or publication of this work. If medical or other expert assistance is required, the services of a competent professional person should be sought.

The web addresses cited in this text were current as of June 2018 unless otherwise noted.

Acquisitions Editor: Diana Vincer; **Senior Developmental Editor:** Cynthia McEntire; **Managing Editor:** Ann C. Gindes; **Copyeditor:** Annette Pierce; **Permissions Manager:** Martha Gullo; **Senior Graphic Designers:** Nancy Rasmus and Joe Buck; **Cover Designer:** Keri Evans; **Cover Design Associate:** Susan Rothermel Allen; **Photo Asset Manager:** Laura Fitch; **Visual Production Assistant:** Joyce Brumfield; **Photo Production Coordinator:** Amy M. Rose; **Photo Production Manager:** Jason Allen; **Senior Art Manager:** Kelly Hendren; **Illustrations:** © Human Kinetics; **Illustrator:** Heidi Richter; **Printer:** Versa Press

Human Kinetics books are available at special discounts for bulk purchase. Special editions or book excerpts can also be created to specification. For details, contact the Special Sales Manager at Human Kinetics.

Printed in the United States of America   10 9 8 7 6 5

The paper in this book is certified under a sustainable forestry program.

Human Kinetics
1607 N. Market Street
Champaign, IL 61820
USA

United States and International
Website: **US.HumanKinetics.com**
Email: info@hkusa.com
Phone: 1-800-747-4457

Canada
Website: **Canada.HumanKinetics.com**
Email: info@hkcanada.com

E6874

I would like to dedicate this book to my children, William, Allison, and Thomas, and to my wife, Lynne. Thank you so much for everything.

- Michael Terry

This book is whole-heartedly dedicated to my wife, Susan. Her presence, ethic and beautiful disposition perpetually inspire and motivate me every second of every day.

- Paul Goodman

CONTENTS

FOREWORD

Let's face it—hockey players are unlike any other athletes in the world. I'm not taking anything away from other types of athletes, but I do think it takes a certain level of skill to fly around an area enclosed by solid, immovable walls, pushing into ice on thin metal blades while wearing extra pounds of equipment and using a stick to handle a tiny puck—all while five opposing players literally try to put you through the glass.

Truth is, hockey players are unique because of the way we *move.* If you are a young player reading this, then you know that from an early age we hockey players are taught to move in unconventional ways to be able to propel ourselves on skates in every direction possible. Unlike running, skating requires speed and power in your quads, glutes, and calves as you push out to the side instead of to the back. Powerful skaters are almost always overdeveloped in these areas, which can help with performance but in the long term can lead to many other issues.

Point is, training your body to be fast, explosive, and powerful without giving up your mobility, athleticism, and longevity has never been more important. I'm sure when you think of hockey, you think of speed and power. Training those skills is the fun part, and it can be easy to neglect your mobility and flexibility. But if you want to be your best for as long as possible, bringing all these different types of training together is crucial. This can become an intricate process. I mean, how can you focus on becoming great at all the on-ice skills if you're preoccupied with a never-ending checklist of off-ice training? Thankfully, that's where my good friends Paul Goodman and Dr. Mike Terry step in.

Dr. Mike Terry has been the orthopedic surgeon for the Chicago Blackhawks for 12 years. Not only has he seen a ton of orthopedic injuries, but he has also seen many recoveries. Comprehension of the human body is one thing, but he takes understanding of the hockey player's anatomy to the next level. Seeing Dr. Terry usually means something has gone seriously wrong, and it's time to take drastic measures to fix it.

On the other hand, your time with Paul Goodman has neither a beginning nor an end. Paul has been the strength coach for the Chicago Blackhawks for nearly the same stretch of time as Dr. Terry has been involved with the team. Work with Paul can range from initial injury prevention and in-season maintenance to off-season peak performance and injury rehabilitation. If you want to be a professional hockey player, you have to put your heart and soul into it. The same can be said for Paul's level of commitment to understanding what makes athletes great. Not only does he help you transform your body, but he also helps you improve your mental, emotional, and spiritual approach to the game.

A lot of people credit our three Stanley Cup championships in Chicago strictly to the players on the ice and, to a certain degree, it is understandably so. But what they fail to see is how many other skilled and gifted people behind the scenes have committed their lives to create that team success that you see on the ice or on television.

Paul and Dr. Terry are great examples of that. They are an amazing duo—not only because of their separate and differing expertise but also because of how they are able to overlap and communicate that knowledge to each other. They are engaged with their players and help us through the process of understanding *why* we do what we do. They want us to ask questions, to learn, to grow.

It's important to learn through your own trial and error when you rise to the top, but sometimes you can take little shortcuts and learn through the failures and successes of other people to get to the next level. This book is a culmination of the years of hard work and hands-on experience of two people who have been working with top athletes for years. In other words, it's a major shortcut, so *use it to your advantage*!

Hockey is a great sport because it constantly challenges you. There is always a new hurdle coming at you that pushes you to adapt, learn, and get better. I wish I had this book when I was much younger because it's a tool I keep returning to which I will use for years to come. Whether you take a lot or a little from this book, never forget that the best players in hockey never stop learning and never stop improving their game.

—Jonathan Toews

THE HOCKEY PLAYER IN MOTION

The game of hockey is evolving. Recent changes in rules and in the interpretation of rules have fostered a faster and more wide-open game. This can be seen at every level of hockey from mite to the NHL and international competition. Speed, skill, and stamina are rewarded now more than ever.

Despite this evolution, some factors remain constant. At all levels, hockey seasons are long and grueling. Young hockey players often play multiple games per day over multiple days during tournaments, and professional athletes often have seasons that can last eight to nine months and include up to 100 games. The combination of athleticism, intelligence, and endurance remains a requirement for hockey players, and improvement of skill and level of play continues to be directly related to training both on and off the ice.

Hockey athletes are changing as well. Hockey players are better suited for today's game than ever before. Athletes are training smarter and including healthy diets and more resources into their training regimens. Hockey athletes no longer show up to training camp to get in shape; elite athletes show up on their first day ready to play and in excellent shape both on and off the ice.

HOCKEY ACTION

The hockey player in motion is unique. Skating alone is a highly technical activity requiring coordination, speed, power, agility, and conditioning in addition to a good deal of skill. When combined with the other activities hockey athletes perform while playing, it becomes clear why hockey is such a challenging sport.

Consider the common activity of skating forward in a straight line. As a hockey player begins to stride forward with the left skate, both the right hip and knee flex. As the skater pushes off with the right lower extremity, the gastrocnemius and soleus muscles fire to extend the ankle, the peroneal muscles fire to stabilize the ankle, the quadriceps muscles fire to extend the knee, and the gluteal muscles fire to extend and abduct the hip (figure 1.1). Simultaneously, the core muscles (figure 1.2) must be fully engaged to stabilize the upper body, and the right upper extremity swings forward as the biceps and pectoralis muscles (figure 1.3) engage and begin to fire.

During this time, the left hip flexors flex the hip, the hamstrings flex the knee, the adductor muscles in the groin pull the left lower extremity in toward the center of the body, and the upper-back and posterior deltoid muscles work to extend the left shoulder. For the left-footed stride, the process begins anew using the muscles on the opposite sides.

This example demonstrates the complexity one of the simplest activities a hockey player performs. The strength of the muscles involved in each portion of the stride governs how fast a skater can skate and how rapidly he or she can accelerate. The skater's power also influences speed and acceleration. Agility is critical for avoiding or creating contact, maneuver-

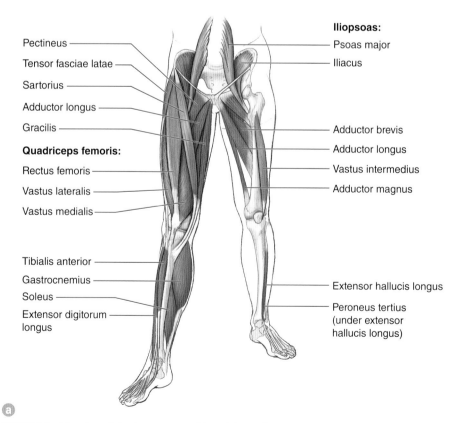

FIGURE 1.1   Muscles of the lower extremities: *(a)* anterior.

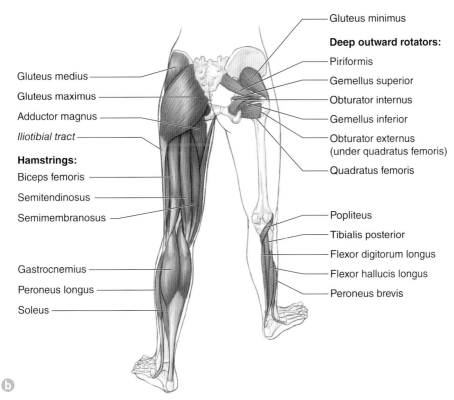

Gluteus minimus

Deep outward rotators:

Piriformis

Gemellus superior

Obturator internus

Gemellus inferior

Obturator externus
(under quadratus femoris)

Quadratus femoris

Popliteus

Tibialis posterior

Flexor digitorum longus

Flexor hallucis longus

Peroneus brevis

Gluteus medius

Gluteus maximus

Adductor magnus

Iliotibial tract

Hamstrings:

Biceps femoris

Semitendinosus

Semimembranosus

Gastrocnemius

Peroneus longus

Soleus

FIGURE 1.1 Muscles of the lower extremities: *(b)* posterior.

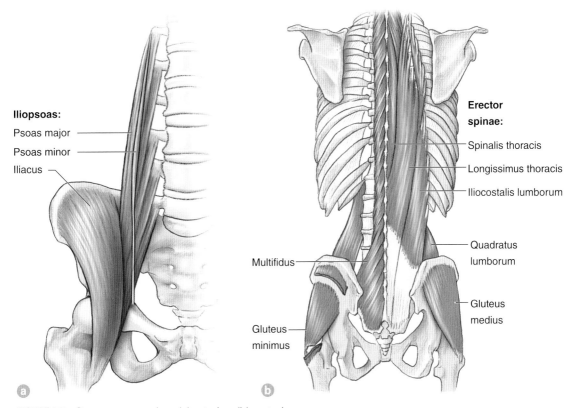

Iliopsoas:

Psoas major

Psoas minor

Iliacus

Erector spinae:

Spinalis thoracis

Longissimus thoracis

Iliocostalis lumborum

Quadratus lumborum

Gluteus medius

Multifidus

Gluteus minimus

FIGURE 1.2 Outer core muscles: *(a)* anterior; *(b)* posterior.

3

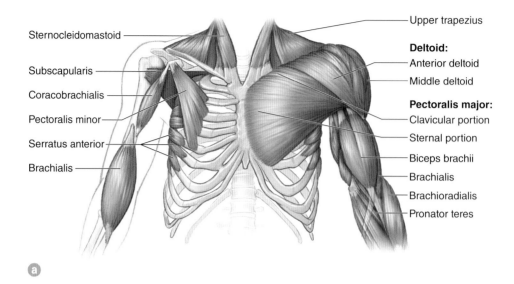

Sternocleidomastoid

Subscapularis

Coracobrachialis

Pectoralis minor

Serratus anterior

Brachialis

Upper trapezius

Deltoid:
Anterior deltoid

Middle deltoid

Pectoralis major:
Clavicular portion

Sternal portion

Biceps brachii

Brachialis

Brachioradialis

Pronator teres

a

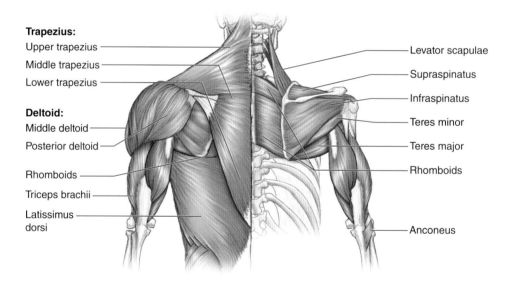

Trapezius:
Upper trapezius

Middle trapezius

Lower trapezius

Deltoid:
Middle deltoid

Posterior deltoid

Rhomboids

Triceps brachii

Latissimus
dorsi

Levator scapulae

Supraspinatus

Infraspinatus

Teres minor

Teres major

Rhomboids

Anconeus

b

FIGURE 1.3 Upper torso: *(a)* anterior; *(b)* posterior.

ing around the ice, and performing the necessary puck skills. Flexibility determines how far a skater can flex the hip and knee to get into a lower tucked position and how much he or she can extend and finish the stride. Balance is critical in every facet of hockey, even in the simple stride, considering that the player needs to remain upright despite moving across a rock-hard, slick sheet of ice while changing directions on razor-sharp blades. Aerobic conditioning affects how long and fast a skater can go.

This quick breakdown of the hockey player in motion demonstrates how physically and physiologically complex playing hockey can be. However, breaking down these complex motions into simpler ones can help focus training techniques and allow us to isolate muscle groups and function in an effort to improve them individually. In the end, this allows a collective improvement that translates to improved performance on the ice.

STRENGTH, POWER, SPEED, AND AGILITY

Strength—resisting or imposing a force—is essential for a variety of reasons and critical to the success of hockey athletes. Strength is required in every battle along the boards, in every stride while skating, in every change of direction on the ice, and in every shot. Stronger athletes won't win every battle, but strength puts them in a better position every time they enter one.

Because strength is the maximum force one can exert on an object, it becomes clear how the stronger athlete has the advantage in a battle along the boards. As two players push against each other on the ice to win the puck, the stronger athlete will move the weaker one as he wishes, if all else is equal, allowing him to win the battle. It may be less clear how strength benefits hockey players in other facets of the game, but if other hockey activities are broken down to the movements required to perform those activities, it becomes clearer.

Skating is a complex activity, but in its most basic deconstruction, it is a series of muscle contractions that generate the force to move the skater across the ice. The stronger those muscle contractions are, the more force they generate and the greater the acceleration of the skater will be. Once again, the stronger athlete has the advantage over the weaker one.

Strength, power, and speed are all interrelated, but it's important to understand the differences between them. Power is the development of force over a period of time. The athlete who can generate the maximum force in the shortest time is the most powerful athlete. This translates into explosiveness on the ice. The more powerful athlete is the more explosive athlete.

Power and explosiveness are beneficial in just about every aspect of hockey as well. When changing direction or taking off for a loose puck, the more powerful athlete will be able to generate his or her maximum force more quickly, which translates to a more explosive first few strides and the advantage over a less powerful athlete. A more powerful goalie will push from post to post faster than a less powerful goalie, allowing him to potentially stop more shots and ready himself quicker, giving him the advantage as well.

A final example of the benefits of power is shooting. A more powerful athlete can generate force on her stick and transmit it to the puck faster than a less powerful one. This allows the more powerful athlete to shoot a harder shot in a shorter time.

Both power and strength are required to generate speed. Speed in hockey is seen clearly in skating. The faster skater has the advantage. Speed is evident in other aspects of the game, however. Stick speed is as important to defensemen, forwards, and goalies as well. Perhaps nowhere is this more easily seen than during the face-off. The player with the fastest stick speed will win more face-offs than his or her slower opponent.

Agility is the ability to perform the required tasks in a coordinated fashion quickly and easily. Agility differentiates a great puck handler from a mediocre one. Agility is required all the time in hockey in other ways, too. Skaters must make coordinated adjustments countless times while moving down the ice. The requirement for agility when skating multiplies while making contact with an opposing player or battling for a puck. Goalies adjust their position multiple times each time the puck is in their zone and often several times during each shot. The more agile athlete will have an advantage in almost all aspects of the game.

CONCLUSION

Throughout *Hockey Anatomy*, strength, power, speed, agility, flexibility, balance, and aerobic conditioning are the focus. Each of these components of fitness and training is required to play the game of hockey at any level, and the improvement of each of these components will improve your game. We provide many exercises and alternatives to improve overall readiness to play hockey in addition to explaining the muscles and skills these exercises target. Muscles are categorized as primary or secondary. Some exercises focus on specific muscle groups and others involve multiple muscle groups. We also highlight the skill or hockey activity the exercise is most likely to be affect.

Primary muscles   Secondary muscles

While exercises are divided into specific categories, there is considerable crossover between categories. Strength, power, and speed are all critically related. Speed, balance, and agility are also intertwined with each other. Aerobic conditioning allows the athlete to be proficient in all athletic endeavors at a higher level for a longer time.

The goal of *Hockey Anatomy* is to provide the tools hockey players need to develop all these athletic characteristics safely and effectively. We hope these exercises provide you with the framework to become the best hockey player you can be.

STRENGTH

Strength in hockey is critical to nearly every activity, from shooting and skating to stopping and battling in corners. Although all hockey players need to be strong to resist the actions of other players and to exert their will when battling other players, strength is needed during noncontact activities, such as skating and shooting, as well.

The exercises in this chapter build muscle strength. You will require a recovery period before working the same group of muscles again. To give the muscles a chance to recover and build, do not do the strength-building work right before skating (in some cases, not even the day before skating). Finally, consider starting with one exercise for each muscle group during your initial workouts and building to multiple exercises for each muscle group after you learn how your body responds and recovers from each one. Remember that form is critical. You won't get the most out of your workouts if your form breaks down, and in some cases you could put yourself at risk for injury.

SINGLE-LEG ISOMETRIC WALL SQUAT

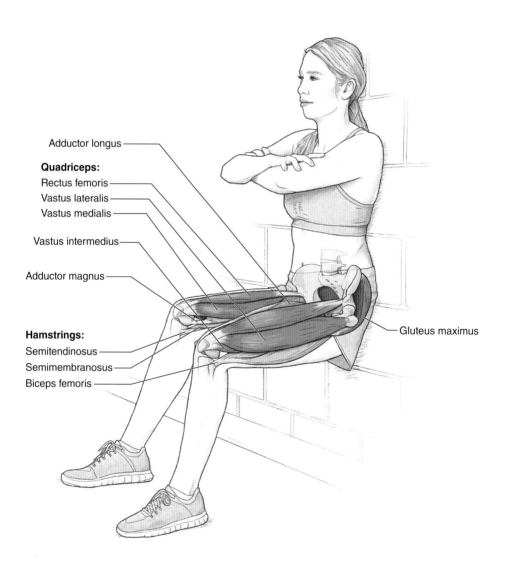

Adductor longus

Quadriceps:
Rectus femoris
Vastus lateralis
Vastus medialis

Vastus intermedius

Adductor magnus

Hamstrings:
Semitendinosus
Semimembranosus
Biceps femoris

Gluteus maximus

Execution

1. Stand with the back and shoulders against a wall, chest upright and tall. Stand with feet 8 to 10 inches (20-25 cm) apart, toes pointing straight ahead.
2. Descend into a squat, maintaining wall contact with the entire back and shoulders.
3. Sink to a depth at which the knees and hips are level or nearly so. Keep the hands off the thighs. The arms can be extended forward and parallel to the floor, kept at the sides, or crossed as shown.
4. Center one foot and lift the other foot off the ground.
5. Hold the bottom position for the allotted time, emphasizing pulling into the squat, and then switch legs.
6. Do not let the hips or the shoulders shift or hike while standing on the single leg.

Muscles Involved

Primary: Quadriceps (rectus femoris, vastus lateralis, vastus medialis, vastus intermedius), gluteus maximus

Secondary: Hamstrings (semitendinosus, semimembranosus, biceps femoris), adductor longus, adductor magnus

HOCKEY FOCUS

This exercise is demanding for the quadriceps muscles. The quadriceps and gluteus maximus are the major muscles used during skating. This exercise strengthens them in a fairly isolated way. It eliminates complex motion and isolates the primary muscles. The exercise starts aerobically, but quickly turns anaerobic, so anticipate lactic acid buildup and the resulting burn. In addition to strengthening critical muscles, you will learn to deal with the burning feeling that occurs on the ice at the end of the shift and control it to some degree. This translates on the ice to helping you establish and maintain a low base and develop the ability to withstand high levels of lactic acid accumulation. The longer you are able to hold the bottom position, the higher the threshold for accumulation you'll be able to handle. This will, in turn, translate to being able to skate in a position with a low center of gravity longer.

VARIATION

Stability Single-Leg Isometric Squat

Perform the single-leg isometric wall squat, but place a stability disc under the planted foot to challenge your stability.

STRENGTH

ZERCHER SQUAT

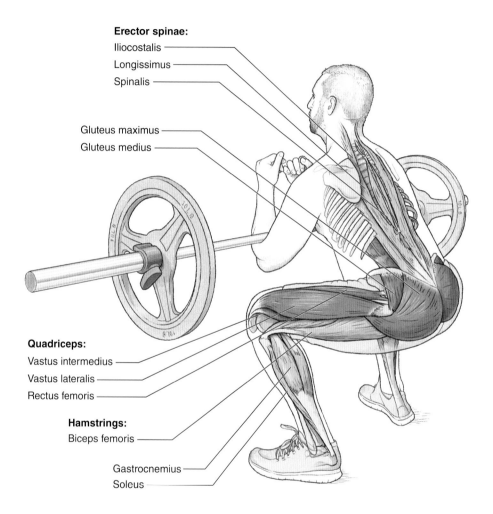

Erector spinae:
Iliocostalis
Longissimus
Spinalis

Gluteus maximus
Gluteus medius

Quadriceps:
Vastus intermedius
Vastus lateralis
Rectus femoris

Hamstrings:
Biceps femoris

Gastrocnemius
Soleus

Execution

1. Walk into a squat rack and place a barbell in the bend of the elbows with hands either clasped or apart. Stand up to raise the weight off the rack and take two small steps back from the squat rack where the safety bars are placed at the appropriate level for the bottom of the squat, which in this exercise is the height which allows the squat to proceed until the hamstrings are just below parallel to the floor. Place the feet just wider than shoulder width and keep them slightly externally rotated.

2. Push the hips back to initiate the squat. While maintaining a straight spine (the head is neither hyperextended nor flexed) lower the bar and body until the hamstrings are below parallel to the floor. Keep the elbows in tight to the body and inhale on the descent.

3. Once the bottom position is reached, keep the inhaled breath in and drive the weight up forcefully by extending the knees and hips.

4. Exhale at the top of the squat and stand tall.

Muscles Involved

Primary: Quadriceps (rectus femoris, vastus lateralis, vastus medialis, vastus intermedius), gluteus maximus, gluteus medius

Secondary: Hamstrings (semitendinosus, semimembranosus, biceps femoris), adductor magnus, adductor longus, adductor brevis, rectus abdominis, erector spinae (iliocostalis, longissimus, spinalis), gastrocnemius, soleus, gracilis

HOCKEY FOCUS

The squat is the foundation for building leg, core, and hip strength through a dynamic movement. By performing the squat through a full range of motion, you will strengthen different regions of the primary muscles and activate the secondary muscles more completely. This will improve range of motion and strength while the body is in different positions (unlike the wall squat). This exercise improves the ability to push throughout the entire skating stride and helps you stay low while skating to improve balance, speed, and the ability to change direction quickly. In addition, your base will be better supported during board battles in which you need to be strong on the skates to withstand external forces.

VARIATION

Sumo Squat

Hold a barbell on the front or back of the shoulders or in the bend of the arms, or hold a single dumbbell in front. Assume a squat stance and widen the base of support. Step the feet out two to three foot widths from shoulder width on each side. Point toes out to the sides. From this widened base, perform the same steps as in the back squat. This base will add stress to the hip adductors and groin.

TRANSVERSE SQUAT

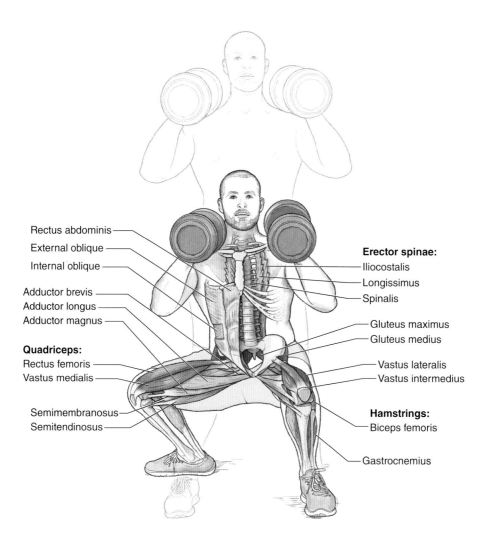

Rectus abdominis

External oblique

Internal oblique

Adductor brevis

Adductor longus

Adductor magnus

Quadriceps:
Rectus femoris

Vastus medialis

Semimembranosus

Semitendinosus

Erector spinae:
Iliocostalis

Longissimus

Spinalis

Gluteus maximus

Gluteus medius

Vastus lateralis

Vastus intermedius

Hamstrings:
Biceps femoris

Gastrocnemius

12

Execution

1. Hold a pair of dumbbells at the shoulders using a neutral parallel grip. Stand tall, then externally rotate one hip, and step out to a 45-degree angle.
2. Descend into a squat once the foot has made contact with the ground. Distribute the weight equally on both legs and bend the knees at the same rate.
3. Even though the leg moves at an angle and steps out, the shoulders should remain fixed straight ahead at the starting position so there is rotation at the hips.
4. Push back up forcefully to the starting position. Step out to the other side with the other leg and repeat for the allotted number of repetitions per side.

Muscles Involved

Primary: Quadriceps (rectus femoris, vastus lateralis, vastus medialis, vastus intermedius), gluteus maximus, gluteus medius

Secondary: Hamstrings (semitendinosus, semimembranosus, biceps femoris), adductor magnus, adductor longus, adductor brevis, rectus abdominis, external oblique, internal oblique, erector spinae (iliocostalis, longissimus, spinalis), gastrocnemius

HOCKEY FOCUS

The transverse squat develops the player's ability to get low and stay low when opening up or pivoting on the ice. These motions are critical when changing direction or transitioning to or from skating backward. These transitional movements are also critical for the majority of goalie movements in the crease, especially when goalies are pushing from one post to the other.

VARIATIONS

Barbell Transverse Squat

Perform the same movement, but place a bar on the upper back and shoulders. The length of the bar through the rotational pattern will increase the torque at the spine.

Low Transverse Squat

Perform the same movement with dumbbells or a barbell, but stay in a low squat during the exercise. Start in the bottom position of the squat with weight at the appropriate position and then rotate one hip and step out at a 45-degree angle, but do not raise the body up or down to do so. Keep tension in the squat the entire time.

Transverse Squat and Press

While performing the transverse squat, press a pair of dumbbells overhead when stepping back to the middle starting stance.

SINGLE-LEG SQUAT

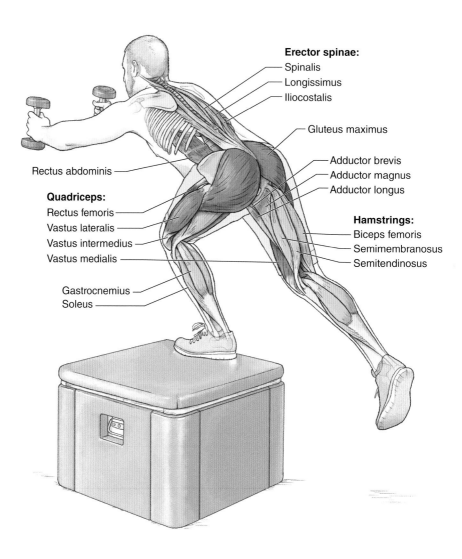

Erector spinae:
Spinalis
Longissimus
Iliocostalis

Gluteus maximus

Adductor brevis
Adductor magnus
Adductor longus

Rectus abdominis

Quadriceps:
Rectus femoris
Vastus lateralis
Vastus intermedius
Vastus medialis

Hamstrings:
Biceps femoris
Semimembranosus
Semitendinosus

Gastrocnemius
Soleus

14

Execution

1. Stand on one leg on a box. The box should be at least as high as the length of your thigh. The opposite leg hangs off the side of the box. Hold a dumbbell in each hand.
2. Bring the dumbbells up to create a 90-degree angle at the elbows.
3. Keeping a straight spine and neutral head position, bring the hips back to initiate the squat. Descend in a controlled manner until the hamstring of the leg squatting is below the knee.
4. Drive back up to the start by extending the knee and hip.
5. Perform all repetitions for one leg and then switch legs.

Muscles Involved

Primary: Quadriceps (rectus femoris, vastus lateralis, vastus medialis, vastus intermedius), gluteus maximus

Secondary: Hamstrings (semitendinosus, semimembranosus, biceps femoris), adductor magnus, adductor longus, adductor brevis, rectus abdominis, erector spinae (iliocostalis, longissimus, spinalis), gastrocnemius, soleus

HOCKEY FOCUS

This exercise develops strength while maintaining balance on a single leg. When in contact, rapidly changing direction, or shooting, the ability to withstand loads placed on a single leg is paramount. Strength is also obtained in the secondary stabilizers and core muscles, which will help while crossing over and changing direction and in contact situations.

VARIATION

Goblet Single-Leg Squat

Hold one kettlebell or dumbbell in the goblet position (in front of chest under chin). Keeping a straight spine and neutral head position, bring the hips back to initiate the squat. Control the descent until the hamstring of the squatting leg is below the knee. Drive back up to the start by extending the knee and hip. Repeat all repetitions for one leg. Perform the exercise on the other leg.

FORWARD–BACKWARD LUNGE

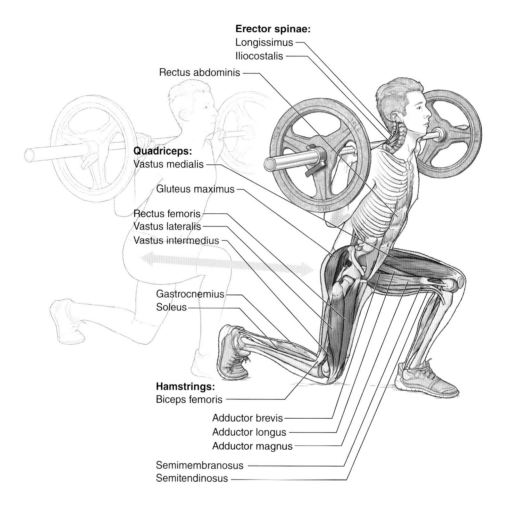

Erector spinae:
Longissimus
Iliocostalis

Rectus abdominis

Quadriceps:
Vastus medialis

Gluteus maximus

Rectus femoris
Vastus lateralis
Vastus intermedius

Gastrocnemius
Soleus

Hamstrings:
Biceps femoris

Adductor brevis
Adductor longus
Adductor magnus

Semimembranosus
Semitendinosus

Execution

1. Place a barbell on the back and upper trapezius or hold a dumbbell in each hand hanging low or at the shoulders.

2. Keeping the chest and back straight, step forward and descend on the lead leg so that the ankle and knee are bent to 90 degrees and the back knee slightly touches the ground.

3. Once the bottom position is achieved, push back and through the starting position to then reach back with the same leg that moved forward. Descend into the reverse lunge, bending the front knee and ankle to 90 degrees and touching the back knee to the ground. Do not rise to perform the backward lunge.

4. Stay low through the transition from front to back and vice versa.

5. Continue in this forward and backward lunging, moving the same leg to the front and back for the allotted number of repetitions before switching to the other leg.

Muscles Involved

Primary: Quadriceps (rectus femoris, vastus lateralis, vastus medialis, vastus intermedius), gluteus maximus

Secondary: Hamstrings (semitendinosus, semimembranosus, biceps femoris), adductor magnus, adductor longus, adductor brevis, gastrocnemius, soleus, erector spinae (iliocostalis, longissimus, spinalis)

HOCKEY FOCUS

Staying low while skating is a coaching cue for any position player. As soon as a player begins to raise the center of gravity, the ability to accelerate, change direction, and decelerate is compromised. This lunging exercise places the player in the low position on a single leg while cycling through the range of motion that is used in a skating stride. Lactic acid will accumulate in the stationary leg, which mimics the burn that is felt in the single leg on the ice. The gains realized during this exercise will help the hockey player stay in a ready position while skating, allowing change of direction or stopping to occur immediately, instead of wasting time returning to the ready position from a taller stance.

VARIATION

Forward–Backward Lunge on BOSU

Keep the planted leg (the leg not moving) on top of a balance trainer such as a BOSU ball. The unstable surface and the height increase the difficulty. Perform in the same manner as if the planted leg were on the floor.

45-DEGREE WALKING LUNGE

Quadriceps:
Vastus intermedius
Vastus medialis
Rectus femoris
Vastus lateralis

Hamstrings:
Biceps femoris
Semimembranosus
Semitendinosus

Gastrocnemius
Soleus

Execution

1. Place a barbell on the back and upper trapezius or hold a dumbbell in each hand hanging low or at the shoulders.
2. With one leg, step forward at a 45-degree angle and lunge.
3. Step forward with the back leg at a 45-degree angle and continue walking in this manner. Keep the shoulders straight ahead; do not rotate at the angle the leg is moving.

Muscles Involved

Primary: Quadriceps (rectus femoris, vastus lateralis, vastus medialis, vastus intermedius), gluteus maximus

Secondary: Hamstrings (semitendinosus, semimembranosus, biceps femoris), adductor magnus, adductor longus, adductor brevis, gastrocnemius, soleus, erector spinae (iliocostalis, longissimus, spinalis)

HOCKEY FOCUS

This exercise strengthens the single leg as the athlete descends, opens up, and mimics the skating stride. The strength gained through this exercise directly benefits the hockey player when pushing off and crossing over. The ability to decelerate from the forward motion during this exercise helps to develop the player's ability to withstand eccentric forces of the skating stride and builds strength rapidly.

VARIATION

Lateral Lunge

Repeat in the same manner as the 45-degree lunge, except this time step directly out to the side. Descend onto the stepping leg so that the knee bends to a 90-degree angle. The stationary leg should remain straight as the movement is performed. Step back to the start and reach out to the opposite side.

SKATER STEP-UP ON BOX

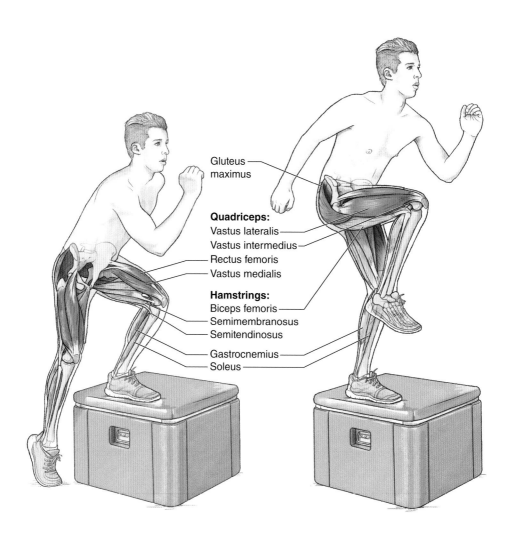

Gluteus maximus

Quadriceps:
Vastus lateralis
Vastus intermedius
Rectus femoris
Vastus medialis

Hamstrings:
Biceps femoris
Semimembranosus
Semitendinosus

Gastrocnemius
Soleus

Execution

1. Stand on top of a box 18 to 24 inches (46-61 cm) high and hang one leg off the side. The arms are free or holding a pair of light dumbbells.

2. Bring the hip of the standing leg back and descend to a quarter-depth squat. Descend until the toes of the moving leg lightly touch the ground. The toes of the moving leg point toward the floor, and the knee is bent to a 45-degree angle.

3. Once the toes touch the ground, immediately change direction, driving the knee up and across the hip toward the chest and back to the start. The arms swing like a sprinter's as the leg drives up and back down.

4. Once the knee is driven up and across, immediately descend again to touch the toes to the floor. Continue in this manner by rapidly changing direction at the top and bottom of the movement.

5. Complete all repetitions on one leg and then switch legs.

Muscles Involved

Primary: Quadriceps (rectus femoris, vastus lateralis, vastus medialis, vastus intermedius), gluteus maximus

Secondary: Hamstrings (semitendinosus, semimembranosus, biceps femoris), adductor magnus, adductor longus, adductor brevis, gastrocnemius, soleus

HOCKEY FOCUS

This exercise develops the ability to drive and to accelerate and decelerate rapidly. This exercise also improves and manages anaerobic tolerance in the standing leg because of the continuous muscle contraction. These attributes can be seen in the player's agility and ability to quickly change direction on the ice.

GOOD MORNING

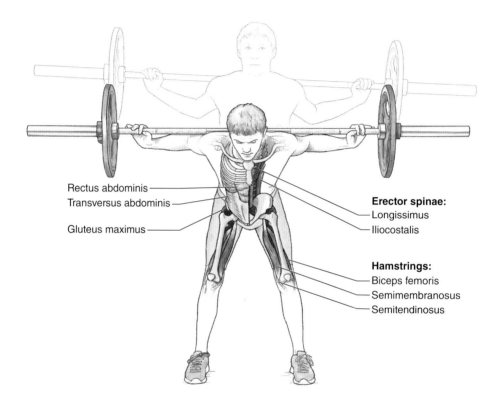

Rectus abdominis

Transversus abdominis

Gluteus maximus

Erector spinae:
Longissimus
Iliocostalis

Hamstrings:
Biceps femoris
Semimembranosus
Semitendinosus

Execution

1. Place a barbell on the upper trapezius. Hold the bar tight, driving the elbows down toward the ribs.

2. Keeping the back flat and shoulders back, bow forward by hinging at the hips. Drive the hips back while maintaining the weight in the center or through the balls of your feet.

3. Lower the chest until it is parallel to the ground or where flexibility allows, ensuring the lower and midback are straight.

4. Raise the chest by driving the hips forward, and assume the standing position without leaning back.

Muscles Involved

Primary: Hamstrings (semitendinosus, semimembranosus, biceps femoris), gluteus maximus, erector spinae (iliocostalis, longissimus, spinalis)

Secondary: Rectus abdominis, transversus abdominis

HOCKEY FOCUS

Strength of the lower back is paramount for maintaining proper posture and deferring fatigue while skating. This exercise strengthens the posterior chain (muscles on the back of the body), which enables the athlete to maintain posture while at the same time counterbalancing the development of the anterior muscles of the leg.

VARIATION

Single-Leg Good Morning

Perform the exercise the same way, except balance on one leg.

SINGLE-LEG ROMANIAN DEADLIFT

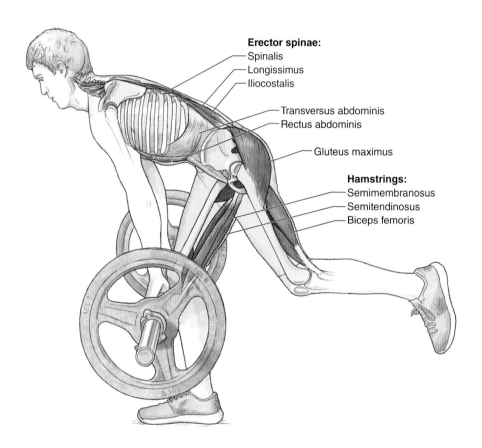

Erector spinae:
Spinalis
Longissimus
Iliocostalis

Transversus abdominis
Rectus abdominis

Gluteus maximus

Hamstrings:
Semimembranosus
Semitendinosus
Biceps femoris

Execution

1. Grasp a barbell with an overhand grip and hold it against the front of the thighs. Stand with the feet hip-width apart, toes pointed straight ahead. Keep the chest upright, back tight, and shoulders pulled back.

2. As you slide the barbell down the front of the legs, balance on one leg. Drive the lifted leg up and back as the weight descends to below the knee or midshin, depending on flexibility.

3. As the barbell slides down, the torso and lifted leg come to parallel with the floor. Do not round the back as the barbell descends; avoid reaching with the bar.

4. To return to standing, extend the hips and drive them forward. Avoid arching the lower back. Lower the lifted leg. Repeat, lifting the opposite leg.

Muscles Involved

Primary: Hamstrings (semitendinosus, semimembranosus, biceps femoris), gluteus maximus, erector spinae (iliocostalis, longissimus, spinalis)

Secondary: Rectus abdominis, transversus abdominis

HOCKEY FOCUS

This exercise strengthens the posterior chain and enhances posture during skating. You also will find yourself able to reach out farther in front during skating while maintaining control. Developing the muscles targeted in this exercise will help prevent injury when skating, battling, and reaching forward. It also helps you perform these activities more forcefully and efficiently. In addition, the ability to balance while bringing the weight down and up works on stabilizing at the hip. This ability enhances proprioceptive capacity, which will transfer directly onto the ice.

NORDIC CURL

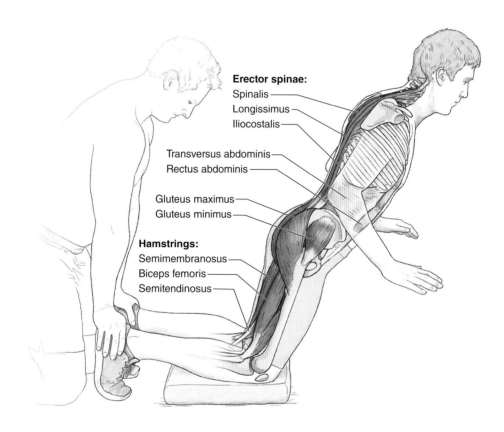

Erector spinae:
Spinalis
Longissimus
Iliocostalis

Transversus abdominis
Rectus abdominis

Gluteus maximus
Gluteus minimus

Hamstrings:
Semimembranosus
Biceps femoris
Semitendinosus

Execution

1. Kneel on a soft mat or balance pad, with the knees directly under the hips. Keep the chest upright, back tight, shoulders back, and hips completely extended. A partner holds your feet down by pushing on the heels or ankles.
2. Slowly, eccentrically fall forward while hinging at the knees and keeping the hips in line with the torso.
3. Lower the body forward as far as possible without falling and then pull back up to the start.

Muscles Involved

Primary: Hamstrings (semitendinosus, semimembranosus, biceps femoris), gluteus maximus, gluteus minimus, erector spinae (iliocostalis, longissimus, spinalis)

Secondary: Rectus abdominis, transversus abdominis

HOCKEY FOCUS

To keep the muscles of the legs balanced, it is important to focus on posterior work to counteract the strength of the quadriceps, which much of the sport emphasizes. This exercise will help the player remain balanced while also working on core stabilization. The significant postural muscle activation during this drill translates to a crossover on the ice regardless of the position the athlete plays on the ice. The posture will aid in keeping the athlete's chest upright and in a proper athletic position. To be an effective skater, the athlete's posture needs to as linear and upright as possible to properly transfer energy from the lower to upper body.

VARIATION

Nordic Curl With Push-Up

Perform the Nordic curl, but lower all the way to the floor and then push up with the arms to return to the start.

STRENGTH

27

BOX HIP BRIDGE

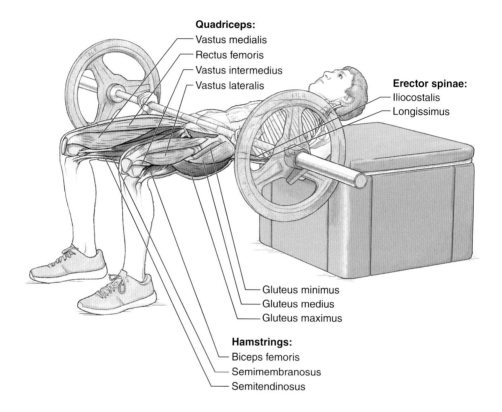

Quadriceps:
Vastus medialis
Rectus femoris
Vastus intermedius
Vastus lateralis

Erector spinae:
Iliocostalis
Longissimus

Gluteus minimus
Gluteus medius
Gluteus maximus

Hamstrings:
Biceps femoris
Semimembranosus
Semitendinosus

Execution

1. Position the upper back and shoulders on a box that is between the height of your lower leg (between the ground and your knee) and 12 inches (30 cm). Place the feet hip-width apart and flat on the floor. Settle the hips on the floor. Grasp a barbell and place it at the crease of the hips.
2. Drive the weight up, keeping it in contact with the hips the entire time by extending the hips.
3. At the top of the lift, the knees should be at 90-degree angles, and the thighs should be in line with the torso.
4. Return the hips to the floor and lightly touch before reengaging and driving the weight back up.

Muscles Involved

Primary: Hamstrings (semitendinosus, semimembranosus, biceps femoris), gluteus maximus, adductor magnus, adductor longus, adductor brevis

Secondary: Erector spinae (iliocostalis, longissimus, spinalis), quadriceps (rectus femoris, vastus lateralis, vastus medialis, vastus intermedius), gluteus medius, gluteus minimus

HOCKEY FOCUS

To accelerate, cross over, and battle along the boards, you need to be in a low athletic position strongly supported by the muscles worked by this exercise. Maintaining a low center of gravity with strength allows you to initiate any athletic movement quickly.

VARIATION

Single-Leg Box Hip Bridge

Perform in the same manner, except balance on one foot.

STAGGERED PUSH-UP

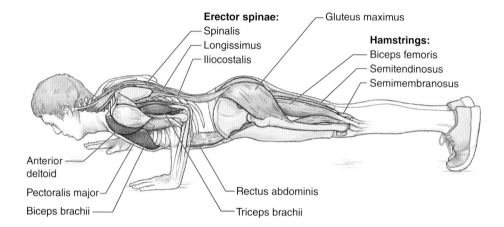

Erector spinae:
Spinalis
Longissimus
Iliocostalis

Gluteus maximus

Hamstrings:
Biceps femoris
Semitendinosus
Semimembranosus

Anterior deltoid

Pectoralis major

Biceps brachii

Rectus abdominis

Triceps brachii

Execution

1. Assume a plank position, with the legs straight and weight on the toes. Place one hand under the shoulder and the other hand several inches in front. Hands are shoulder-width apart.

2. Keeping the body in a straight line from head to heels, lower the body and lightly touch the chest to the ground.

3. Push the body up by pressing into the floor with the hands and extending the elbows.

4. Push all the way to straight arms. Repeat. After completing the allotted repetitions on one side, switch hands and repeat.

Muscles Involved

Primary: Pectoralis major, triceps brachii, anterior deltoid

Secondary: Rectus abdominis, erector spinae (iliocostalis, longissimus, spinalis), gluteus maximus, hamstrings (semitendinosus, semimembranosus, biceps femoris), biceps brachii

HOCKEY FOCUS

The push-up is where all upper-body strength should begin. Correct positioning and execution of this movement leads to more complex and higher-intensity exercises. This exercise teaches you how to track the elbows and engage the core to maintain a straight line with the body. Upper-body pressing strength will help you shoot, skate, and battle more effectively. The core muscle control achieved with this exercise will also be helpful in every aspect of the game.

HIP BRIDGE WITH ALTERNATING KETTLEBELL PRESS

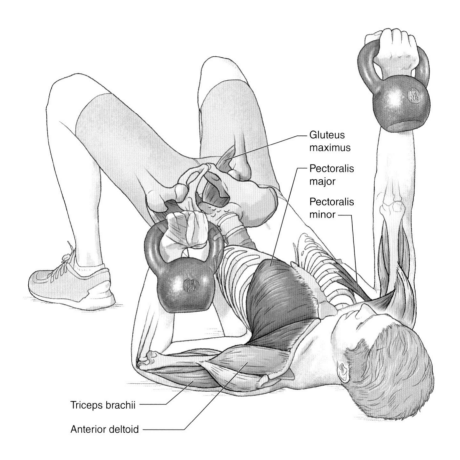

Gluteus maximus

Pectoralis major

Pectoralis minor

Triceps brachii

Anterior deltoid

Execution

1. With kettlebells in hand, lie on the ground with the feet flat and under the knees.
2. Bridge the hips up as high as possible and maintain that position throughout the lift.
3. Press both kettlebells toward the ceiling, keeping the back and hips on the ground and extending the elbows.
4. In a controlled manner, bring one kettlebell down to the chest and push it back up to the starting position. Bring the other kettlebell down and up.

Muscles Involved

Primary: Pectoralis major, pectoralis minor

Secondary: Triceps brachii, anterior deltoid, gluteus maximus

HOCKEY FOCUS

Pushing and fending off another player requires both the upper body to be stable and strong and requires you to use your upper extremities independently. This develops neuromuscular control of the arms independently of one another. To perform this exercise efficiently, the single arm must balance the weight and be able to control it as it descends. Track the arm close to the body; it should not flare out to the side as the weight descends and ascends. This will teach the correct pattern and the most advantageous way to drive weight and prevent putting the shoulder in a position where it will be vulnerable to injury. In addition, performing the bridge and press at the same time requires the glutes to fire to stabilize the lower body.

PULL-UP WITH KNEES UP

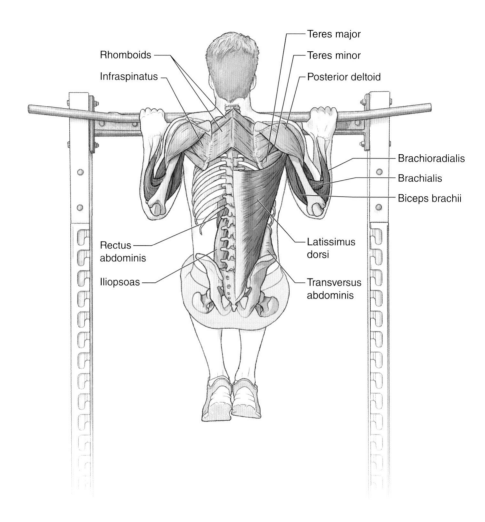

Rhomboids

Infraspinatus

Teres major

Teres minor

Posterior deltoid

Brachioradialis

Brachialis

Biceps brachii

Rectus abdominis

Iliopsoas

Latissimus dorsi

Transversus abdominis

Execution

1. Grasp a pull-up bar with an overhand (palms down) grip and hang straight down.
2. While hanging, bring the knees up toward the chest, creating 90-degree angles at the hips and knees.
3. While holding this position, pull the body up and raise the chin above the bar.
4. Maintain the leg position during the pull-up and lowering movements.
5. The descent of the pull-up should be controlled. Lower the body until the arms completely lock out.

Muscles Involved

Primary: Latissimus dorsi, biceps brachii, brachialis, brachioradialis

Secondary: Posterior deltoid, rhomboids, rectus abdominis, teres major, teres minor, infraspinatus, transversus abdominis, iliopsoas

HOCKEY FOCUS

When protecting or shooting the puck, the back plays a vital role in producing force and stabilizing the core and the shoulders. Holding the knees up removes the compensatory swing of the legs out during the pull-up. In addition, the core and hip flexors (iliopsoas) are maximally activated in this position. Both are key components in stride recovery and increasing speed.

VARIATION

Alternative Grips

Athletes can perform the pull-up with knees up using a neutral grip (palms facing one another), reverse grip (palms turned up), or alternate grip (one palm up and the other down).

SUPINE ROW

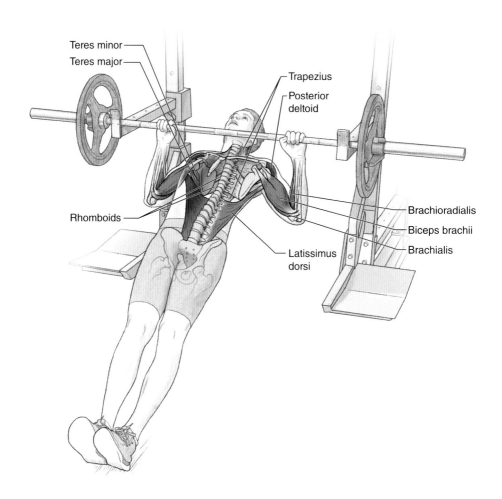

Teres minor

Teres major

Trapezius

Posterior deltoid

Rhomboids

Brachioradialis

Biceps brachii

Brachialis

Latissimus dorsi

Execution

1. Lie on your back under a barbell or suspension trainer, with your feet together with legs straight. Grasp the bar with an overhand grip and straight arms. The bar should be set so that your back is 6 inches (15 cm) off the floor at the top of the lift.
2. As you lift your body, drive the hips up and keep the head back so there is a straight line from heels to head.
3. Pull the chest up to the barbell or between the suspension trainer handles.
4. Control the descent from the top position, maintaining the straight line.

Muscles Involved

Primary: Latissimus dorsi, posterior deltoid, biceps brachii, brachialis, brachioradialis

Secondary: Rhomboids, trapezius, teres major, teres minor, infraspinatus

HOCKEY FOCUS

Straight-arm play is often fatiguing. Because the upper extremity is extended, strength is imperative. Whether reaching for a puck or defending with one arm while maintaining or gaining puck possession along the boards, strength in the upper back and posterior deltoid is critical. It enables you to withstand the external forces pushing and pulling against you while stabilizing the shoulder with the upper extremity extended away from the body.

KETTLEBELL SQUAT AND PRESS

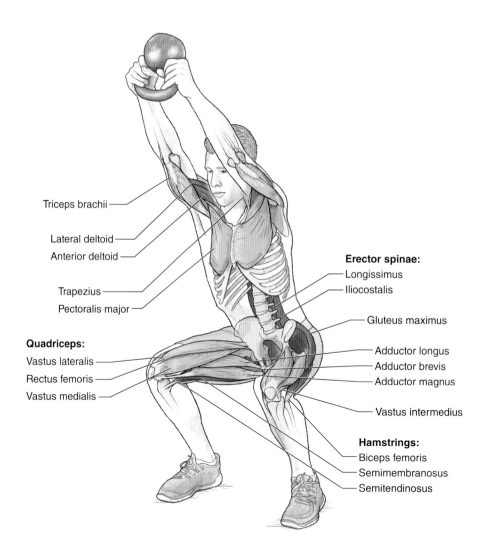

Triceps brachii

Lateral deltoid

Anterior deltoid

Trapezius

Pectoralis major

Erector spinae:
Longissimus
Iliocostalis

Gluteus maximus

Quadriceps:
Vastus lateralis
Rectus femoris
Vastus medialis

Adductor longus
Adductor brevis
Adductor magnus

Vastus intermedius

Hamstrings:
Biceps femoris
Semimembranosus
Semitendinosus

Execution

1. Grasp a kettlebell with both hands on the handles and flip the bell up so the bottom is toward the ceiling. Hold the kettlebell at chest height. Assume a traditional squat base in which the feet are just outside of shoulder width and slightly externally rotated.
2. Descend into the squat. At the same time, press the kettlebell up until the arms are fully extended. End with the hamstrings below parallel.
3. Ascend from the squat, bringing the kettlebell back to chest height.

Muscles Involved

Primary: Gluteus maximus, hamstrings (semitendinosus, semimembranosus, biceps femoris), anterior deltoid, lateral deltoid, erector spinae (iliocostalis, longissimus, spinalis)

Secondary: Quadriceps (rectus femoris, vastus lateralis, vastus medialis, vastus intermedius), adductor longus, adductor magnus, adductor brevis, triceps brachii, trapezius, posterior deltoid, pectoralis major

HOCKEY FOCUS

This exercise activates and strengthens muscles throughout the body and works them through a range of motion while requiring stabilization and balance. The keys to this movement are to press the kettlebell to complete lockout overhead while descending into a deep squat and to avoid leaning forward to do so. For hockey, the entire body needs to work as a unit stabilizing from external forces throughout a complete range of motion.

VARIATION

Alternative Leg Positions

Athletes can also perform the kettlebell squat and press from a sumo squat base or a split squat stance.

HALF-KNEELING SINGLE-ARM DUMBBELL PRESS WITH TWIST

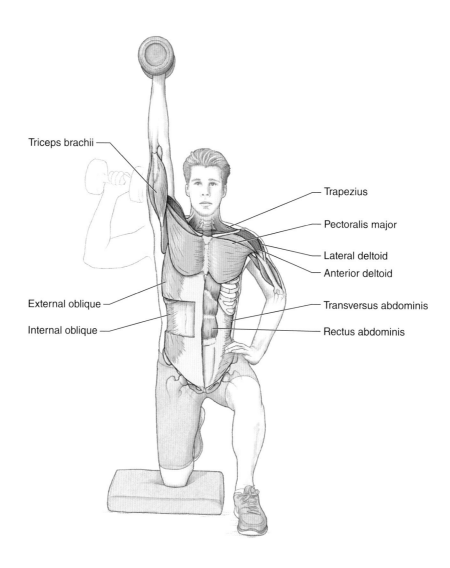

Triceps brachii

Trapezius

Pectoralis major

Lateral deltoid

Anterior deltoid

External oblique

Transversus abdominis

Internal oblique

Rectus abdominis

Execution

1. Lunge into a split position with the back knee on the floor and the front knee bent at 90-degrees at both the knee and hip. Place a soft pad under the knee on the floor.
2. Grab a dumbbell with the hand opposite the front leg (if the left leg is in front, the right hand holds the dumbbell).
3. Bring the dumbbell to the shoulder and hold it in a pronated grip (palm turned away from the body). Place the other hand on the hip of the front leg.
4. Press the dumbbell overhead, twisting it so that the palm rotates in toward the body.
5. Bring the dumbbell down to the shoulder, again twisting it to a pronated grip.
6. Complete all repetitions on one side and then switch sides.

Muscles Involved

Primary: Anterior deltoid, lateral deltoid

Secondary: Triceps brachii, trapezius, posterior deltoid, pectoralis major, rectus abdominis, transversus abdominis, external oblique, internal oblique

HOCKEY FOCUS

This exercise focuses on unilateral shoulder strength and contralateral stabilization. In hockey, shooting and single-arm stick play both rely on a strong shoulder through the entire motion while the opposite side of the body remains stable.

POWER

Power is work applied over a distance, but it is also energy expended over time. It uses the player's strength and translates to explosiveness. Building power improves skating ability. Power is what allows the skater to start, stop, and accelerate quickly. Power is what allows the hockey player to win battles. Powerful actions expend significant energy when performed for long durations. Training with this in mind allows you to work hard over longer periods.

Power exercises require significant recovery time after workouts (in most cases more recovery time than strength exercises do), so they should be spaced appropriately with at least two days between power exercise days. The power muscle groups pull something toward the body or push it away, propel the body forward, and propel the body upward. Because the power exercises use multiple muscle groups, multiple muscle groups may require rest for recovery. Similar to the strength exercises, take care to plan these workouts around competition so that muscles are not sore or incapacitated when needed for performance.

WAVE SQUAT

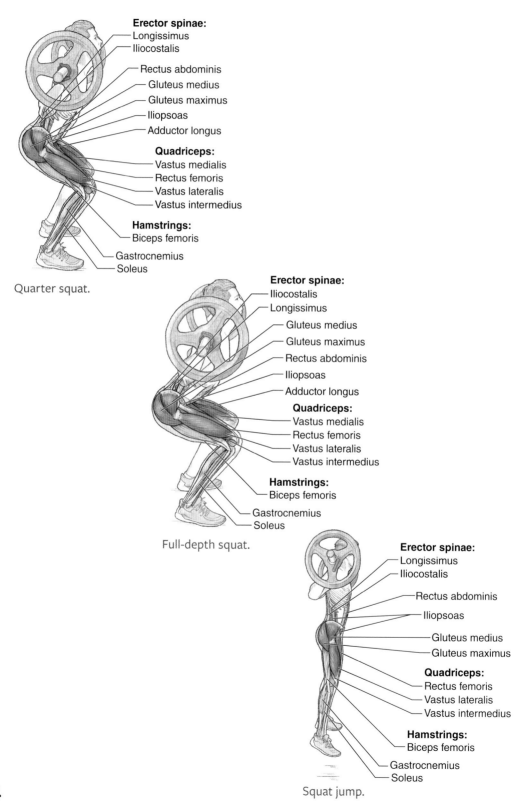

Erector spinae:
Longissimus
Iliocostalis

Rectus abdominis
Gluteus medius
Gluteus maximus
Iliopsoas
Adductor longus

Quadriceps:
Vastus medialis
Rectus femoris
Vastus lateralis
Vastus intermedius

Hamstrings:
Biceps femoris

Gastrocnemius
Soleus

Quarter squat.

Erector spinae:
Iliocostalis
Longissimus

Gluteus medius
Gluteus maximus
Rectus abdominis
Iliopsoas
Adductor longus

Quadriceps:
Vastus medialis
Rectus femoris
Vastus lateralis
Vastus intermedius

Hamstrings:
Biceps femoris

Gastrocnemius
Soleus

Full-depth squat.

Erector spinae:
Longissimus
Iliocostalis

Rectus abdominis
Iliopsoas
Gluteus medius
Gluteus maximus

Quadriceps:
Rectus femoris
Vastus lateralis
Vastus intermedius

Hamstrings:
Biceps femoris

Gastrocnemius
Soleus

Squat jump.

Execution

1. Walk into a squat rack and place a barbell behind the neck along the shoulders. Stand up to raise the weight off the rack and take two small steps back from the squat rack. The feet are just wider than shoulder width and slightly externally rotated.

2. Descend into a quarter squat by pushing the hips back and until the knees bend about 20 degrees.

3. Repeat two more quarter squats.

4. Perform one full-depth squat, in which the hamstrings are parallel to the ground at the completion of the descent.

5. Ascend from the full squat and perform one full-depth squat jump. Land softly.

6. The three quarter-depth squats, one full squat, and one full-squat jump equal one wave. Repeat for the allotted number of waves.

Muscles Involved

Primary: Quadriceps (rectus femoris, vastus lateralis, vastus medialis, vastus intermedius), gluteus maximus, gluteus medius

Secondary: Hamstrings (semitendinosus, semimembranosus, biceps femoris), adductor magnus, adductor longus, adductor brevis, rectus abdominis, erector spinae (iliocostalis, longissimus, spinalis), gastrocnemius, soleus, iliopsoas

HOCKEY FOCUS

The ability to withstand the buildup of lactic acid levels in the legs and yet still be explosive is vital to the sport of hockey. You need to be able to handle the accumulation and still be as effective as when the shift or game began. This combination version of the squat enables you, regardless of position, to replicate that feeling and continue to be explosive. In addition, it teaches the body to flush the lactic acid quickly when performed under timed rest intervals to emulate what is experienced on the ice.

HEIDEN SQUAT

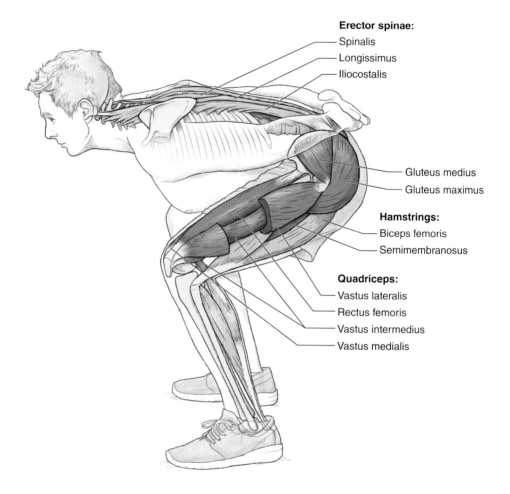

Erector spinae:
Spinalis
Longissimus
Iliocostalis

Gluteus medius
Gluteus maximus

Hamstrings:
Biceps femoris
Semimembranosus

Quadriceps:
Vastus lateralis
Rectus femoris
Vastus intermedius
Vastus medialis

Execution

1. Assume a squat base with feet shoulder-width apart.
2. Lower the chest until it is parallel to the ground.
3. Clasp the hands behind the back at the lumbar spine.
4. Keeping the chest down, squat by bending the knees to lower the body.
5. Descend and ascend rapidly during each squat.

Muscles Involved

Primary: Quadriceps (rectus femoris, vastus lateralis, vastus medialis, vastus intermedius), gluteus maximus, gluteus medius

Secondary: Hamstrings (semitendinosus, semimembranosus, biceps femoris), erector spinae (iliocostalis, longissimus, spinalis), gastrocnemius, soleus

HOCKEY FOCUS

Hockey, and specifically skating, relies on joint angles. The Heiden squat puts the lower extremities into an extreme position. It enables the body to accumulate high levels of lactic acid and bend correctly at the hips, knees, and ankles at the same time. The chest-down position limits the range of motion in order to keep stress on the lower limbs. It also strengthens the lower lumbar spine, which maintains proper skating posture when the chest is brought upright.

VARIATION

Lateral Heiden Squat

Assume the same starting position as the Heiden squat. On each squat, step slightly out to the side to widen the base and then return to the starting stance.

HIGH–LOW SPEED SQUAT

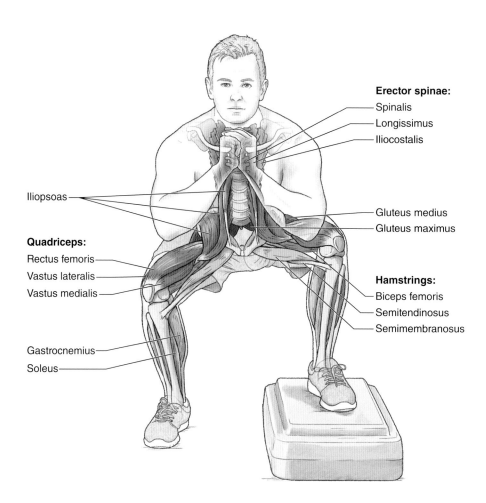

Erector spinae:
Spinalis
Longissimus
Iliocostalis

Iliopsoas

Gluteus medius
Gluteus maximus

Quadriceps:
Rectus femoris
Vastus lateralis
Vastus medialis

Hamstrings:
Biceps femoris
Semitendinosus
Semimembranosus

Gastrocnemius
Soleus

Execution

1. Place a 6- to 10-inch (16-25 cm) box under one foot.

2. Assume a squat stance in which the feet are 10 to 12 inches (25-30 cm) apart. Clasp your hands in front at chest height or behind your back.

3. Keeping your chest up and your spine and head in a neutral position, rapidly descend into a squat and then immediately change direction and ascend from the squat.

4. Do not pause at either the top or the bottom of the squat.

5. Perform the allotted number of repetitions, and then move the box under the other foot and repeat.

Muscles Involved

Primary: Quadriceps (rectus femoris, vastus lateralis, vastus medialis, vastus intermedius), gluteus maximus, gluteus medius, iliopsoas

Secondary: Hamstrings (semitendinosus, semimembranosus, biceps femoris), erector spinae (iliocostalis, longissimus, spinalis), gastrocnemius, soleus

HOCKEY FOCUS

The elevation of one leg in the high–low speed squat emphasizes the stress placed on that leg, thereby accumulating more lactic acid and increasing the threshold in that leg. In addition, the rapid acceleration and deceleration movement develops speed in the contraction. On the ice, this translates into a faster turnover while skating.

POWER

HANG HIGH PULL

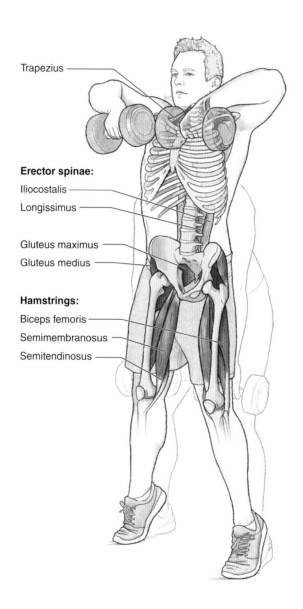

Trapezius

Erector spinae:

Iliocostalis

Longissimus

Gluteus maximus

Gluteus medius

Hamstrings:

Biceps femoris

Semimembranosus

Semitendinosus

Execution

1. Hold a pair of dumbbells or a barbell against the legs at hip height with the arms straight. Feet are shoulder-width apart with toes pointing straight ahead.
2. Keeping the shoulders back and the back flat, lower the weight by hinging and pushing the hips back. Support the weight of the body on the middle to the back of the feet. Bring the weight down to the top of the knees.
3. Raise the weight by pushing into the floor and driving the hips forward and up. Extend the ankles by elevating off the heels. As the weight rises to hip height, pull on the weight, driving the elbows up and shrugging the shoulders. Ensure the weight travels directly in front of the body. Do not throw the weight forward with a straight arm or bend the elbows back. The weight should reach chin height. Return to the starting position by bringing the heels down and straightening the arms.
4. Immediately lower the weight to the knees and repeat for the allotted number of repetitions.

Muscles Involved

Primary: Gluteus maximus, gluteus medius, hamstrings (semitendinosus, semimembranosus, biceps femoris)

Secondary: Trapezius, erector spinae (iliocostalis, longissimus, spinalis)

HOCKEY FOCUS

The hang high pull is a foundational power movement that all of the more complex Olympic lifts can develop from. This drill teaches correct athletic position for hockey and propulsion of force into the ground, which in turn translate into more force onto the ice. This is important for initiation speed when both skates are on the ice and you need to generate force to accelerate from a dead stop.

VARIATIONS

High Pull Alternatives

- Perform the hang high pull using a clean (shoulder-width) or snatch (wide) grip.
- Jump off the floor as you pull on the bar.
- When using dumbbells, perform the hang high pull with one arm only or alternating arms.
- Use a sumo squat base.

HANG SNATCH

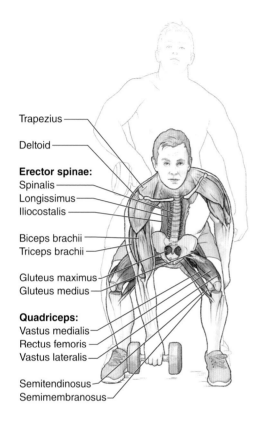

Trapezius

Deltoid

Erector spinae:
Spinalis
Longissimus
Iliocostalis

Biceps brachii
Triceps brachii

Gluteus maximus
Gluteus medius

Quadriceps:
Vastus medialis
Rectus femoris
Vastus lateralis

Semitendinosus
Semimembranosus

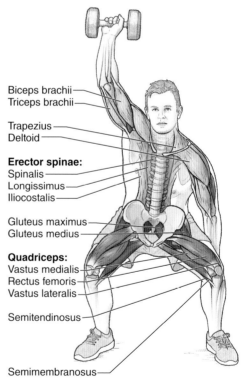

Biceps brachii
Triceps brachii

Trapezius
Deltoid

Erector spinae:
Spinalis
Longissimus
Iliocostalis

Gluteus maximus
Gluteus medius

Quadriceps:
Vastus medialis
Rectus femoris
Vastus lateralis

Semitendinosus

Semimembranosus

Execution

1. Hold a single dumbbell against the front of the leg with the arm straight. Stand with feet shoulder-width apart and toes pointed straight ahead.

2. Keeping the back flat and shoulders back, lower the dumbbell between the legs to below the knees by hinging the hips back. Once the weight reaches this point, push against the floor with the feet and extend the hips and ankles by driving them forward and up. Pull on the dumbbell.

3. As the dumbbell passes the hips, jump off the floor and simultaneously shrug the arm with the dumbbell, elevating the elbow. Do not throw the weight forward with a straight arm.

4. As the weight ascends along the chest and reaches its highest point, the body descends under the weight. As you descend, fully extend the arm so it completely straightens and the weight is locked out overhead.

5. Lower the weight to the shoulder and then down to the starting position. Do not let the weight fall straight down with a straight arm.

Muscles Involved

Primary: Gluteus maximus, gluteus medius, quadriceps (rectus femoris, vastus lateralis, vastus medialis, vastus intermedius), semitendinosus, semimembranosus

Secondary: Trapezius, erector spinae (iliocostalis, longissimus, spinalis), biceps brachii, triceps brachii, deltoid

HOCKEY FOCUS

The hang snatch is a total-body power movement in which the energy generated by the force into the ground is delivered throughout the body and ultimately to a locked out position with the weight overhead. The hang snatch develops the triple-extension power of the ankle, knee, and hip and improves dynamic stabilization of the shoulder when the weight is raised overhead. These qualities are important in hockey because of the need to be strong when extending the arm for slapshots and reaching with the stick.

VARIATIONS

Cross-Body Hang Snatch

Perform the hang snatch, but as the weight descends at the beginning of the movement, bring the weight to the outside of the opposite knee, rotating the torso.

Alternating Hang Snatch

Use two dumbbells and alternate arms on every repetition or every set.

SPEED RUSSIAN LUNGE

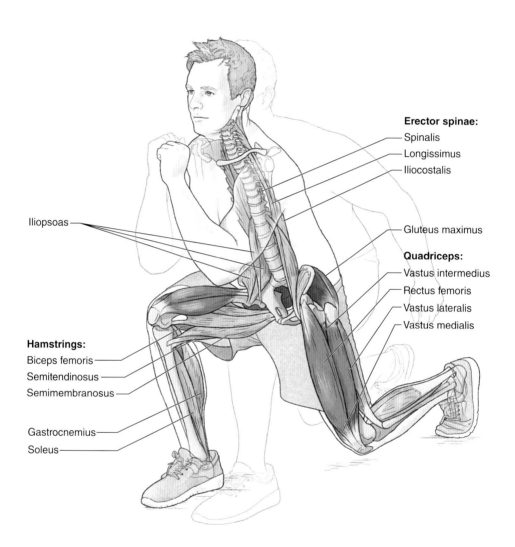

Erector spinae:
Spinalis
Longissimus
Iliocostalis

Iliopsoas

Gluteus maximus

Quadriceps:
Vastus intermedius
Rectus femoris
Vastus lateralis
Vastus medialis

Hamstrings:
Biceps femoris
Semitendinosus
Semimembranosus

Gastrocnemius
Soleus

Execution

1. Assume an exaggerated split stance in which the front knee is at 90 degrees and the back knee extends to about 120 degrees.
2. Staying as low as possible (do not elevate the shoulders; keep them on the same plane in the low position), switch the legs explosively.
3. Pause for a short count and switch again.
4. Perform the allotted number of repetitions per side or for a specific amount of time. The key is to perform the leg switch as quickly as possible, not to finish the set as fast as possible.

Muscles Involved

Primary: Quadriceps (rectus femoris, vastus lateralis, vastus medialis, vastus intermedius), gluteus maximus

Secondary: Hamstrings (semitendinosus, semimembranosus, biceps femoris), adductor magnus, adductor longus, adductor brevis, gastrocnemius, soleus, erector spinae (iliocostalis, longissimus, spinalis), iliopsoas

HOCKEY FOCUS

The ability to recover and switch the legs under the body quickly while staying low is necessary to skate efficiently and explosively. The speed Russian lunge teaches and develops that skill. In addition, staying low throughout the repetitions develops an ability to withstand lactic acid accumulation. This translates to a skater who can maintain speed of movement while delaying fatigue.

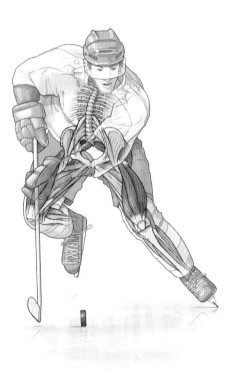

PUSH PRESS

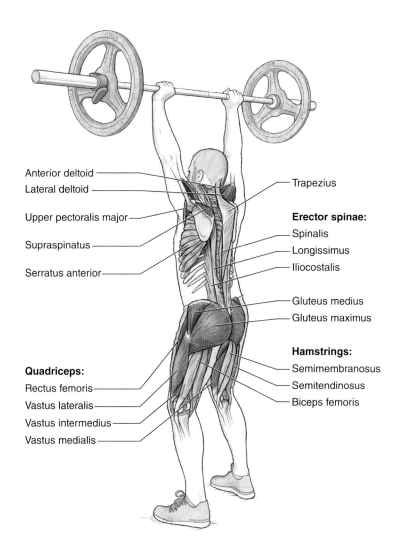

Anterior deltoid

Lateral deltoid

Upper pectoralis major

Supraspinatus

Serratus anterior

Quadriceps:

Rectus femoris

Vastus lateralis

Vastus intermedius

Vastus medialis

Trapezius

Erector spinae:

Spinalis

Longissimus

Iliocostalis

Gluteus medius

Gluteus maximus

Hamstrings:

Semimembranosus

Semitendinosus

Biceps femoris

Execution

1. Position a barbell across the front of the shoulders. Stand with the feet hip-width apart.

2. Keeping the feet flat, slightly bend the knees to lower the body. Immediately counter the movement downward by driving up with the hips.

3. As the hips are extending, push the bar off the shoulders straight overhead. The heels will come off the ground because of the force of the extension of the lower body, but place them back on the ground as soon as the bar is locked out overhead. The momentum and drive from the lower body should project the weight overhead with speed.

4. In a controlled manner, lower the bar to the shoulders and repeat for the allotted number of repetitions.

Muscles Involved

Primary: Quadriceps (rectus femoris, vastus lateralis, vastus medialis, vastus intermedius), gluteus maximus, gluteus medius, anterior deltoid, lateral deltoid, supraspinatus

Secondary: Hamstrings (semitendinosus, semimembranosus, biceps femoris), erector spinae (iliocostalis, longissimus, spinalis), trapezius, upper pectoralis major, serratus anterior

HOCKEY FOCUS

The vertical movement of the push press is a total-body developer. It is beneficial for shoulder stability but also in developing power in the hips. The ability to generate power quickly from a descent to ascent and vice versa translates to more powerful checking and counter hits.

VARIATIONS

Push Press Alternatives

- Perform on a single leg.
- Perform with dumbbells held in a neutral grip in both hands.
- Perform with a single arm.

SKATE HOPS

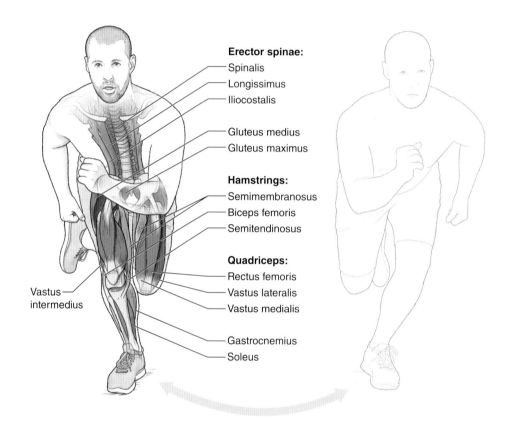

Erector spinae:
Spinalis
Longissimus
Iliocostalis

Gluteus medius
Gluteus maximus

Hamstrings:
Semimembranosus
Biceps femoris
Semitendinosus

Quadriceps:
Rectus femoris
Vastus lateralis
Vastus medialis

Gastrocnemius
Soleus

Vastus intermedius

SAFETY TIP: At first, jump laterally with minimal distance and height until you have mastered the movement.

Execution

1. Stand on one leg with the opposite leg off the ground and slightly behind the support leg.
2. Slightly flex the hip and knee of the planted leg to lower the body.
3. At the bottom of the descent, immediately push off the ground laterally.
4. Land softly on the foot opposite the pushing leg and descend into the same position with flexed hip and knee as initiated in the first jump.
5. Immediately jump back to the first leg and continue the allotted number of repetitions per leg or for a specified time.

Muscles Involved

Primary: Quadriceps (rectus femoris, vastus lateralis, vastus medialis, vastus intermedius), gluteus maximus, gluteus medius

Secondary: Hamstrings (semitendinosus, semimembranosus, biceps femoris), erector spinae (iliocostalis, longissimus, spinalis), gastrocnemius, soleus

HOCKEY FOCUS

This power exercise is another multiple-muscle exercise and is beneficial in many ways. It develops the power used for pushing forward on the ice through the skate. The lateral bound develops the power used in stopping and changing direction.

Once you have gained competency in the skate hop, you can increase the intensity and modify the focus. For example, perform the jump for maximum height and distance. The shoulders will elevate and descend based on the height of the jump. Or perform the jump for maximum distance but not height. The shoulders will stay at the same level throughout the jump.

VARIATIONS

Lateral Bound

Perform the skate hop, but push off and land on the opposite leg and then plant the first leg again and continue pushing laterally in the same direction for the allotted number of repetitions.

Skate Hops With BOSU

Advanced athletes may begin with the planted foot on an unstable surface such as a BOSU ball. Perform the jumps in the same manner, but land on solid ground on one side and land on the unstable surface on the other. Alternatively, perform the jumps and land on an unstable surface on both sides.

KNEE-DRIVE WITH BENCH

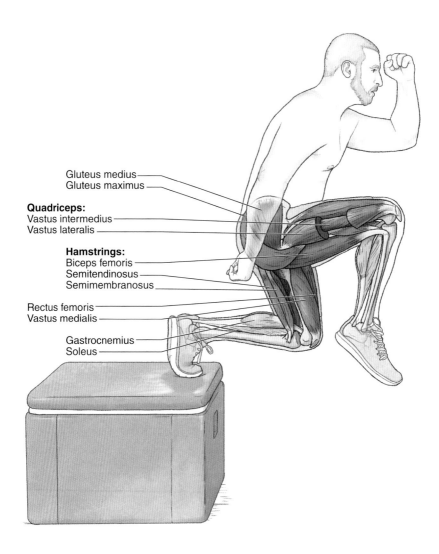

Gluteus medius
Gluteus maximus

Quadriceps:
Vastus intermedius
Vastus lateralis

Hamstrings:
Biceps femoris
Semitendinosus
Semimembranosus

Rectus femoris
Vastus medialis

Gastrocnemius
Soleus

Execution

1. Assume a normal split stance in which the front knee is bent 90 degrees, the back knee is bent at 90 degrees, and the back foot is elevated on a bench.

2. Descend into the split position by flexing the front knee. At the bottom of the descent, immediately push up vertically off the front leg by extending at the hip and knee.

3. At the top of the jump, drive the knee on that side toward the chest. Immediately descend into the split squat and drive up again off the lead leg. Make sure the chest is upright, and use the arms to propel upward.

4. Continue for the allotted number of repetitions for each leg.

Muscles Involved

Primary: Quadriceps (rectus femoris, vastus lateralis, vastus medialis, vastus intermedius), hamstrings (semitendinosus, semimembranosus, biceps femoris), gluteus maximus, gluteus medius

Secondary: Gastrocnemius, soleus

HOCKEY FOCUS

This exercise develops single-leg power and, if performed for a longer duration, anaerobic endurance. This is beneficial for repetitive bursts of speed while under duress. The nature of the sport requires the ability to generate power off a single leg. In addition, driving the knee up on each jump transfers onto the ice by increasing your ability to and the speed at which you bring the knee up and under the center of mass on each successive stride. The quicker and more powerful the drive, the faster you will skate.

VARIATION

Knee-Drive With Bench and Lateral Hop Over Barrier

Set a minihurdle or medicine ball to one side of the lead foot. With the back foot on a bench or box, perform the knee-drive jump. After landing, jump laterally back and forth over the minihurdle or medicine ball.

DEPTH JUMP TO BOX

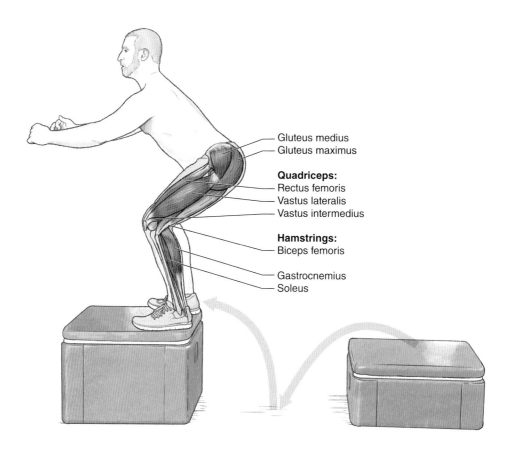

Gluteus medius
Gluteus maximus

Quadriceps:
Rectus femoris
Vastus lateralis
Vastus intermedius

Hamstrings:
Biceps femoris

Gastrocnemius
Soleus

Execution

1. Stand on the edge of a box 12 to 24 inches (30-61 cm) high.
2. Lift one foot and hover over the edge of the box.
3. Drop off the box, landing on two feet. Do not jump up to fall from the box.
4. After making contact with the floor, immediately jump up and onto a box of greater height (12 to 24 inches higher) than the drop-off box.

Muscles Involved

Primary: Quadriceps (rectus femoris, vastus lateralis, vastus medialis, vastus intermedius), gluteus maximus, gluteus medius, gastrocnemius, soleus

Secondary: Hamstrings (biceps femoris, semimembranosus, semi-tendinosus)

HOCKEY FOCUS

This exercise develops power both for pushing off and stopping. The ability to quickly stabilize and react to ground contact leads to a quicker propulsion on each stride on the ice. The stabilization aspect of the drill teaches you to remain under control with a tight core and posture to maximize the transfer of energy from the descent to the ascent. The deceleration aspect of the drop also helps you control the eccentric contraction, which translates to quicker stopping times and quicker reacceleration.

BOX DROP CATCH PLYO PUSH-UP

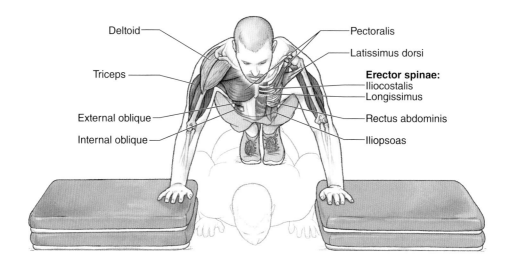

Deltoid

Pectoralis

Latissimus dorsi

Triceps

Erector spinae:
Iliocostalis
Longissimus

External oblique

Rectus abdominis

Internal oblique

Iliopsoas

Execution

1. Position two 4- to 12-inch (10-30 cm) boxes just wider than shoulder-width apart. Assume a push-up position with one hand on each box. At the top of the push-up, lock the arms.
2. Release the hands from the boxes and drop the upper body to the floor. Before the chest hits the ground, bring the hands under and catch the body with the chest about 2 inches (5 cm) off the ground.
3. Hold for two counts, then push off the ground forcefully.
4. Land with the hands on the boxes in the starting position.

Muscles Involved

Primary: Pectoralis, triceps brachii, rectus abdominis, external oblique, internal oblique, erector spinae (iliocostalis, longissimus, spinalis)

Secondary: Latissimus dorsi, deltoid, iliopsoas

HOCKEY FOCUS

This plyometric push-up is another great exercise to develop power for battling, checking, and fighting off an opponent. The exercise and its variations engage the core and hip flexors more than the reactive barbell bench press and its variations.

VARIATION

Staggered Plyo Push-Up

Assume a push-up position with the hands shoulder-width apart and staggered under the body: one hand slightly above the shoulder (closer to the head) and the other slightly below the shoulder (closer to the waist). Descend into the push-up, bringing the chest toward the ground. Before the chest touches the ground, push back up explosively, leaving the ground and rising as high as possible. While in the air, switch the hands that were forward and back. Land on the hands and immediately descend into the next repetition.

ALTERNATING SINGLE-ARM MEDICINE BALL TOSS ON BOSU

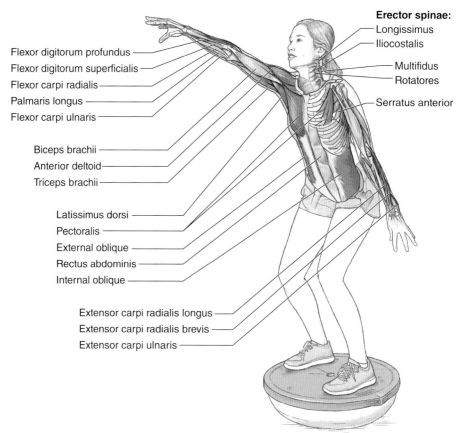

Flexor digitorum profundus
Flexor digitorum superficialis
Flexor carpi radialis
Palmaris longus
Flexor carpi ulnaris

Biceps brachii
Anterior deltoid
Triceps brachii

Latissimus dorsi
Pectoralis
External oblique
Rectus abdominis
Internal oblique

Extensor carpi radialis longus
Extensor carpi radialis brevis
Extensor carpi ulnaris

Erector spinae:
Longissimus
Iliocostalis

Multifidus
Rotatores

Serratus anterior

Execution

1. Place a stability trainer, such as a BOSU ball, with the round side down, and stand on it facing a wall. Hold a medicine ball in one hand.
2. From outside at chest height, throw the medicine ball as hard as possible into the wall. After contacting the wall, the medicine ball will bounce back fast.
3. Immediately catch the medicine ball with the opposite hand and lower it toward the outside of the chest. Throw the ball back to the wall.
4. Continue for the allotted number of repetitions per arm.

Muscles Involved

Primary: Pectoralis, anterior deltoid, latissimus dorsi, external oblique, internal oblique, extensor carpi radialis longus, extensor carpi radialis brevis, extensor carpi ulnaris

Secondary: Multifidus, rotatores, serratus anterior, biceps brachii, triceps brachii, flexor carpi radialis, palmaris longus, flexor carpi ulnaris, flexor digitorum superficialis, flexor digitorum profundus, rectus abdominis, external oblique, internal oblique, erector spinae (iliocostalis, longissimus, spinalis)

HOCKEY FOCUS

This single-arm plyometric drill is important for battling when caught along the boards with one hand on the stick and the other pushing the opponent, trying to move him off the puck. This drill aids in the development of single-arm force and power, but when both hands are on the stick, the culmination is even greater. Power will be generated from the rotation of the core transmitting explosiveness to the shoulder and arm motions, leading to a more powerful transfer of force

through the core to the upper extremities and creating harder, faster, shots. Depending on skill, training goals, and timing in the training program, athletes can perform this exercise on the ground instead of on a stability trainer and from a single leg, with or without the stability trainer.

PLYO PULL-UP

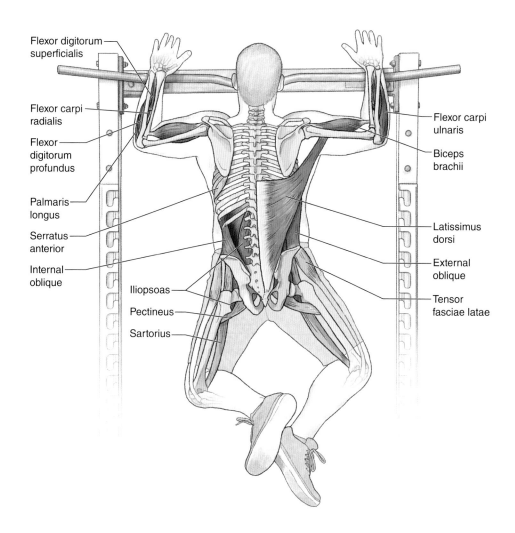

Flexor digitorum superficialis

Flexor carpi radialis

Flexor digitorum profundus

Palmaris longus

Serratus anterior

Internal oblique

Iliopsoas

Pectineus

Sartorius

Flexor carpi ulnaris

Biceps brachii

Latissimus dorsi

External oblique

Tensor fasciae latae

Execution

1. Grasp a pull-up bar with an overhand (palms down) grip and hang straight down.
2. Pull the body up to raise the chin above the bar.
3. The pulling motion should be forceful enough that the hands leave the bar.
4. Once the hands "jump off" the bar, immediately grab it again and descend in a controlled manner to the starting position.
5. Continue for the allotted number of repetitions.

Muscles Involved

Primary: Latissimus dorsi, biceps brachii, flexor carpi radialis, palmaris longus, flexor carpi ulnaris, flexor digitorum superficialis, flexor digitorum profundus, rectus abdominis, external oblique, internal oblique, iliopsoas

Secondary: Serratus anterior, tensor fasciae latae, pectineus, sartorius

HOCKEY FOCUS

The plyo pull-up will help develop power for battling, checking, and shooting. The exercise works grip strength so you will be stronger when shooting. Activating the core will also make you more stable and tougher to knock off the puck. Connecting the core to an upper-body power movement is crucial in hockey. Being stable while at the same time engaging in an upper-body movement is necessary when battling for position. It is also important for goalies, who must make saves while pushing laterally yet keeping an upright posture.

VARIATION

Alternate Hand Grips

The plyo pull-up can be performed with a neutral grip (palms facing one another), reverse grip (palms facing up), or alternate grip (one palm up and the other down).

REACTIVE BARBELL BENT-OVER ROW

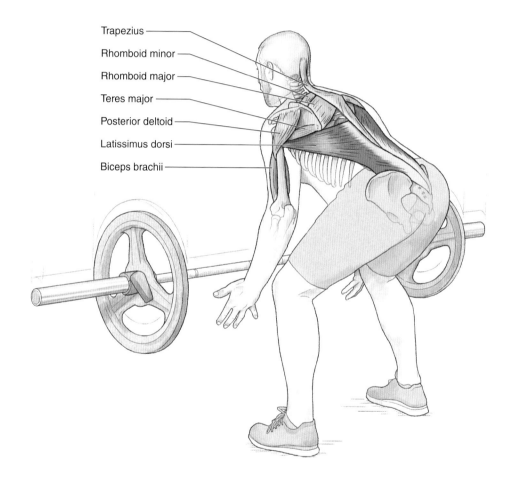

Trapezius

Rhomboid minor

Rhomboid major

Teres major

Posterior deltoid

Latissimus dorsi

Biceps brachii

Execution

1. Grab a barbell with either a reverse grip (palms facing up) or a standard grip (palms facing down). With a slight knee bend and while keeping the back completely flat, lower the barbell to below the knees by bending at the waist between 70 and 90 degrees.

2. Pull the barbell up to the chest line. Stop the barbell and hold it against the chest for one count.

3. Release the barbell from the hands then reach down and catch it before it hits the ground.

4. Immediately pull the barbell back up to the chest and pause before performing the next repetition.

Muscles Involved

Primary: Latissimus dorsi

Secondary: Trapezius, rhomboid major, rhomboid minor, teres major, posterior deltoid, biceps brachii

HOCKEY FOCUS

The reactive barbell bent-over row develops strength and power in pulling, which is important for shooting, battling, and maintaining an athletic position with proper posture while skating or standing in the crease. It is also vital to incorporate ballistic and strength exercises to help develop the muscles that stabilize the shoulder.

VARIATION

Reactive Dumbbell Row

Assume a deep lunge position. Using a neutral grip, hold a dumbbell with the hand opposite the front leg. Place the hand without the dumbbell on top of the knee of the front leg. Row the dumbbell to the ribs and pause for one count. Release the dumbbell from the hand, and then reach down and catch it. Immediately pull it back up to the ribs and pause before performing the next repetition.

SPEED

Speed is defined as the rate of motion. In hockey, speed determines who gets to the puck first, whether or not a player gets loose on a breakaway, and who controls the play. The faster hockey player can break away from his opponent or get back to disrupt his opponent's breakaway. Speed can help a skater recover from a lapse of judgement or allow her to cover more ground (cheat up) without being exposed. The major muscles involved in creating skating speed are the gluteal muscles (gluteus maximus, gluteus medius, and gluteus minimus), hamstrings (semitendinosus, semimembranosus, biceps femoris), quadriceps (rectus femoris, vastus lateralis, vastus medialis, vastus intermedius), and the core muscles, including the rectus abdominis, internal and external obliques, and erector spinae (iliocostalis, longissimus, spinalis).

WALL MARCH

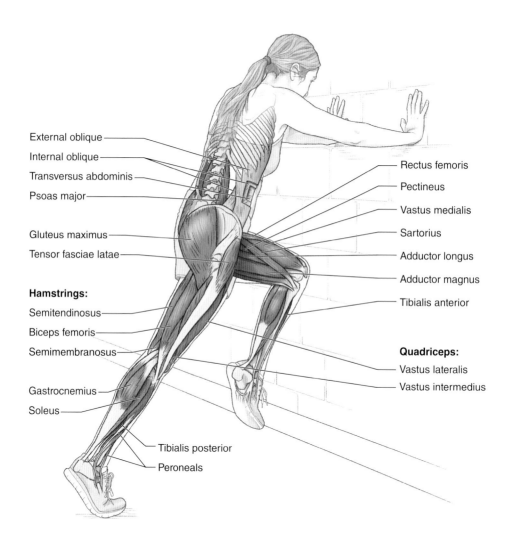

External oblique

Internal oblique

Transversus abdominis

Psoas major

Gluteus maximus

Tensor fasciae latae

Hamstrings:

Semitendinosus

Biceps femoris

Semimembranosus

Gastrocnemius

Soleus

Tibialis posterior

Peroneals

Rectus femoris

Pectineus

Vastus medialis

Sartorius

Adductor longus

Adductor magnus

Tibialis anterior

Quadriceps:

Vastus lateralis

Vastus intermedius

Execution

1. Place hands shoulder-width apart on a wall.
2. Walk the feet back to make a 45-degree angle to the wall from shoulders to toes, keeping the hips in line.
3. Bring one knee up to hip height. The other foot is on the ground with the heel up and the ball of the feet on the ground.
4. On a command or when ready, immediately switch the legs so the standing leg drives up and the opposite leg drives down.
5. Emphasize a hard pull-up and push-down, creating as much force as possible in each direction.
6. On the next command, immediately switch the legs again.
7. Pause and separate each stride.
8. Repeat for the allotted number of repetitions per side or for time.

Muscles Involved

Primary: Quadriceps (rectus femoris, vastus lateralis, vastus medialis, vastus intermedius), hamstrings (semitendinosus, semimembranosus, biceps femoris), gluteus maximus, gastrocnemius, soleus, tibialis posterior, peroneals, tibialis anterior, psoas major, iliacus, tensor fasciae latae, sartorius, adductor longus, adductor brevis, adductor magnus, pectineus

Secondary: Internal oblique, external oblique, transversus abdominis

HOCKEY FOCUS

The ability to switch the legs as fast as possible while creating force into the ground will propel a player very quickly in the direction of choice. In skating, the extension of the hip in the propulsion phase comes from creating a large amount of force and applying it to the ice, but in addition to that, the legs need to rapidly move under the body to recover the stride into the next stride. This drill emphasizes that exchange by instilling an immediate response and quick exchanges.

VARIATIONS

1-2-3 Wall March

Perform the wall march, but exchange the feet rapidly for three strides before pausing. Be sure to drive forcefully up and down into the ground.

Wall March Run

Perform this the same way as the wall march, but switch the legs rapidly in a running fashion, keeping the hips and body in a straight line.

MEDICINE BALL ACCELERATION CHEST PASS

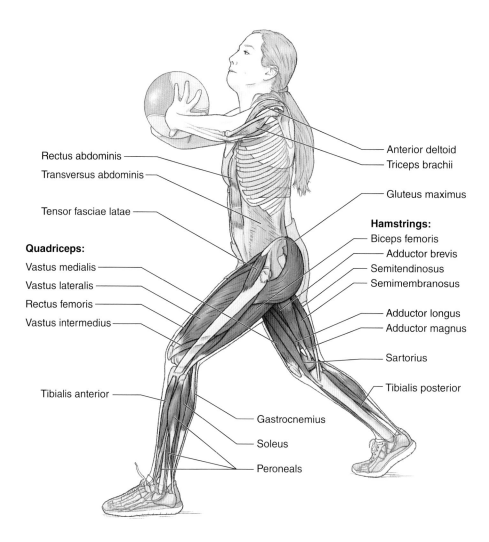

Rectus abdominis

Transversus abdominis

Tensor fasciae latae

Quadriceps:

Vastus medialis

Vastus lateralis

Rectus femoris

Vastus intermedius

Tibialis anterior

Anterior deltoid

Triceps brachii

Gluteus maximus

Hamstrings:

Biceps femoris

Adductor brevis

Semitendinosus

Semimembranosus

Adductor longus

Adductor magnus

Sartorius

Tibialis posterior

Gastrocnemius

Soleus

Peroneals

Execution

1. Stand 3 to 10 yards (2.7-9.1 m) away from a wall or a partner, depending on the program design.
2. Get into a skate-starting stance or a straight-ahead two-point stance. Hold a soft medicine ball (one that does not bounce too much) at chest height.
3. Immediately push off with the lead leg and drive toward the wall or partner.
4. Take one to three powerful strides and chest pass the medicine ball toward the wall or partner as hard as possible.
5. Immediately receive the ball back, backpedaling to the start. Repeat for the allotted number of repetitions per side.

Muscles Involved

Primary: Quadriceps (rectus femoris, vastus lateralis, vastus medius, vastus intermedius), hamstrings (semitendinosus, semimembranosus, biceps femoris), gluteus maximus, gastrocnemius, soleus, tibialis posterior, peroneals, tibialis anterior, psoas major, iliacus, tensor fasciae latae, sartorius, adductor longus, adductor brevis, adductor magnus, pectineus

Secondary: Rectus abdominis, transversus abdominis, anterior deltoid, triceps brachii

HOCKEY FOCUS

Being the first to the puck is a priority in the game. The ability to drive into the ground or ice and accelerate as quickly and in the shortest distance possible will increase overall speed. Developing acceleration and power off a dead stop are necessary for creating space between one player and another.

VARIATIONS

Acceleration Chest Pass With 180-Degree Spin

Stand with your back to a wall or partner. Spin 180 degrees and then move the feet to accelerate in the direction opposite the one you were originally facing and throw the medicine ball to the wall or your partner.

Acceleration Chest Pass With Partner

A partner stands in front of you or to your side. While in a starting stance, catch a pass from your partner and then immediately perform the acceleration strides.

Medicine Ball Acceleration Overhead Pass

Perform the medicine ball acceleration chest pass or any of the variations by throwing the medicine ball overhead.

FALLING START

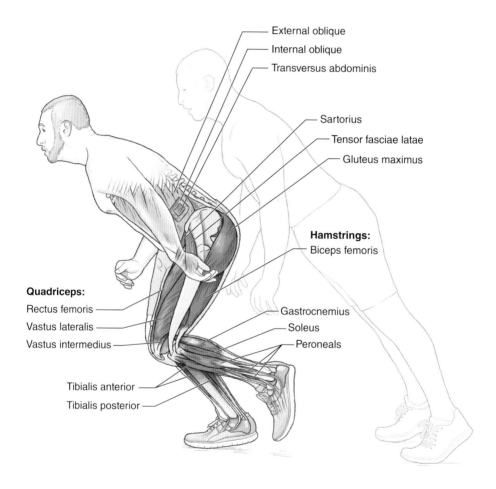

External oblique

Internal oblique

Transversus abdominis

Sartorius

Tensor fasciae latae

Gluteus maximus

Hamstrings:
Biceps femoris

Quadriceps:

Rectus femoris

Vastus lateralis

Vastus intermedius

Gastrocnemius

Soleus

Peroneals

Tibialis anterior

Tibialis posterior

Execution

1. Stand with the feet parallel and hip-width apart.

2. On a command or when ready, lean forward as far as possible (falling), keeping the hips in line with the shoulders and legs.

3. Just before you lose balance, plant one foot into the ground, landing on the ball of that foot about 8 to 12 inches (20-30 cm) in front of you. Accelerate to a full sprint.

4. The goal is to fall as far as possible and then accelerate as quickly as possible, first using short strides and then lengthening them as you gain speed.

5. Move the feet under the body to gather ground quickly.

6. Do not step back with one foot to begin accelerating forward.

Muscles Involved

Primary: Quadriceps (rectus femoris, vastus lateralis, vastus medius, vastus intermedius), hamstrings (semitendinosus, semimembranosus, biceps femoris), gluteus maximus, gastrocnemius, soleus, tibialis posterior, peroneals, tibialis anterior, psoas major, iliacus, tensor fasciae latae, sartorius, adductor longus, adductor brevis, adductor magnus, pectineus

Secondary: Internal oblique, external oblique, transversus abdominis

HOCKEY FOCUS

This acceleration exercise is a reactionary drill to get the feet moving and gather ground as quickly as possible. The ability to move the feet and propel oneself in the direction of choice will aid in separation on the ice. A player must be able to control the body in space and still be able to move quickly. When a player is hit or loses balance, it is important for the player to be able to regain balance and move with speed.

VARIATIONS

Partner Falling Start

With a partner's hands on your shoulders, lean as far as possible into the person holding you up. Without a cue, the partner releases you. Immediately gain your balance and propel forward into a full sprint.

Falling Start Change of Direction

Perform a falling start with or without a partner. After a couple of strides, plant one foot in the ground and either sprint diagonally, immediately stop and backpedal, shuffle laterally to the right or left, or crossover run to the right or left.

BALL DROP

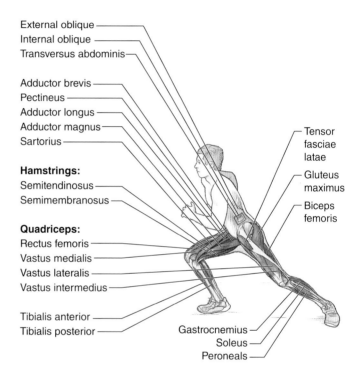

External oblique
Internal oblique
Transversus abdominis

Adductor brevis
Pectineus
Adductor longus
Adductor magnus
Sartorius

Hamstrings:
Semitendinosus
Semimembranosus

Quadriceps:
Rectus femoris
Vastus medialis
Vastus lateralis
Vastus intermedius

Tibialis anterior
Tibialis posterior

Tensor
fasciae
latae

Gluteus
maximus

Biceps
femoris

Gastrocnemius
Soleus
Peroneals

Execution

1. Assume a skater or sprinter stance while facing a partner, who is about 5 yards (4.6 m) away.
2. Your partner holds a tennis ball in each hand out to the sides.
3. Without giving a cue, your partner releases one of the tennis balls. React to the dropped ball and immediately accelerate to catch it before the second bounce.

Muscles Involved

Primary: Quadriceps (rectus femoris, vastus lateralis, vastus medius, vastus intermedius), hamstrings (semitendinosus, semimembranosus, biceps femoris), gluteus maximus, gastrocnemius, soleus, tibialis posterior, peroneals, tibialis anterior, psoas major, iliacus, tensor fasciae latae, sartorius, adductor longus, adductor brevis, adductor magnus, pectineus

Secondary: Internal oblique, external oblique, transversus abdominis

HOCKEY FOCUS

Because reading and reacting to stimulus on the ice are vital in hockey, it is important to develop visual recognition and the ability to accelerate based on that recognition to a space or to the puck. This skill is especially important during face-off draws or as a play is developing.

FLYING

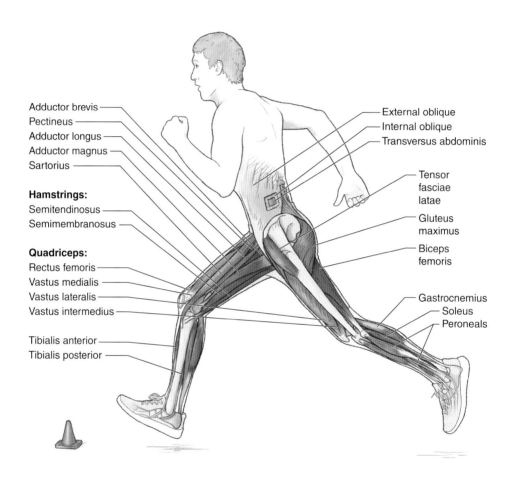

Adductor brevis

Pectineus

Adductor longus

Adductor magnus

Sartorius

Hamstrings:

Semitendinosus

Semimembranosus

Quadriceps:

Rectus femoris

Vastus medialis

Vastus lateralis

Vastus intermedius

Tibialis anterior

Tibialis posterior

External oblique

Internal oblique

Transversus abdominis

Tensor fasciae latae

Gluteus maximus

Biceps femoris

Gastrocnemius

Soleus

Peroneals

Execution

1. Assume a two-point starting stance with the feet staggered.
2. On a command or when ready, begin to jog forward.
3. Gradually build up speed until you hit a marker on the ground or on a verbal or visual command to run at full speed.
4. Continue to run at top speed until you hit another marker or are signaled to decelerate. You can alter the length of the build-up and the length of the sprint as your fitness level and level of comfort with the exercise improve.
5. Be sure you have plenty of room to decelerate.

Muscles Involved

Primary: Quadriceps (rectus femoris, vastus lateralis, vastus medius, vastus intermedius), hamstrings (semitendinosus, semimembranosus, biceps femoris), gluteus maximus, gastrocnemius, soleus, tibialis posterior, peroneals, tibialis anterior, iliopsoas, tensor fasciae latae, sartorius, adductor longus, adductor brevis, adductor magnus, pectineus

Secondary: Internal oblique, external oblique, transversus abdominis

HOCKEY FOCUS

A player *will* experience multiple changes of tempo when playing. It is important to be able to change tempo and achieve maximum speed as quickly as possible, but it is also important to improve that top speed. This type of overspeed training develops stride length off the ice, thereby enhancing speed on the ice.

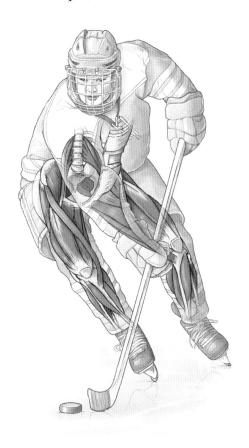

LATERAL RESISTANCE RELEASE

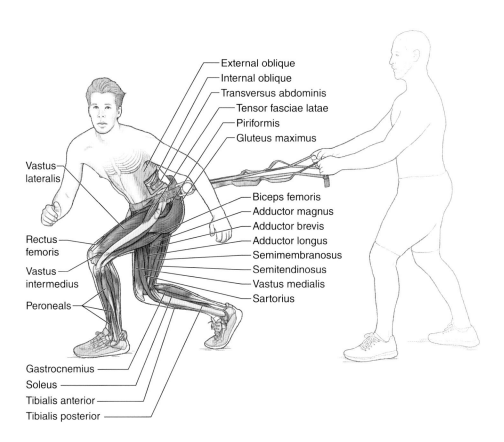

External oblique
Internal oblique
Transversus abdominis
Tensor fasciae latae
Piriformis
Gluteus maximus

Vastus lateralis

Biceps femoris
Adductor magnus
Adductor brevis
Adductor longus
Semimembranosus
Semitendinosus
Vastus medialis
Sartorius

Rectus femoris

Vastus intermedius

Peroneals

Gastrocnemius
Soleus
Tibialis anterior
Tibialis posterior

Execution

1. Loop a resistance band through a belt or a harness. A partner holds the ends of the band while standing beside you.

2. Assume a skater or regular starting stance.

3. Your partner applies tension to the band before the drill begins to avoid jerking you.

4. On command, immediately shuffle or crossover step to top speed against the resistance.

5. At a designated distance, your partner releases the band. Accelerate

free of the resistance for another given distance by either turning the hips and running straight ahead, continuing the lateral shuffle or crossover in the same direction you were going, or spinning the hips 180 degrees and then continuing to shuffle or cross over.

6. To avoid creating a towing effect, the partner must not apply too much resistance to the band. You should be able to keep a good starting position even with the resistance of the band.

Muscles Involved

Primary: Quadriceps (rectus femoris, vastus lateralis, vastus medius, vastus intermedius), hamstrings (semitendinosus, semimembranosus, biceps femoris), gluteus maximus, gastrocnemius, soleus, tibialis posterior, peroneals, tibialis anterior, psoas major, iliacus, tensor fasciae latae, sartorius, adductor longus, adductor brevis, adductor magnus, pectineus, piriformis

Secondary: Internal oblique, external oblique, transversus abdominis

HOCKEY FOCUS

When players are bumped or prevented from going where they want to go on the ice, it is important that they be able to drive through that resistance and then explode past their opponent and gain ice quickly. This movement can take place linearly or laterally at any time. This skill is vital for goalies as well. As movement takes them across the crease, they need to overcome that momentum and immediately push back across or to another position in the crease.

VARIATIONS

Linear Resistance Release

Face a partner whose hands are on your shoulders. Upon initiation of the drill, with a good body lean, run against the resistance of your partner, gathering ground forward. Without a cue, the partner releases you from the resistance by stepping aside. Accelerate as quickly as possible and run through a designated distance. You can also perform this using band resistance at your back.

Reverse Resistance Release

Face away from the direction you will be moving. Run backward against the resistance of your partner. Once you reach a mark and the resistance is released, turn 180 degrees and continue to run or turn 90 degrees and shuffle or cross over. The free shuffle and crossover can be followed by a turn and sprint or a stop and backpedal.

GROUND START

Erector spinae:
- Iliocostalis
- Longissimus
- Spinalis

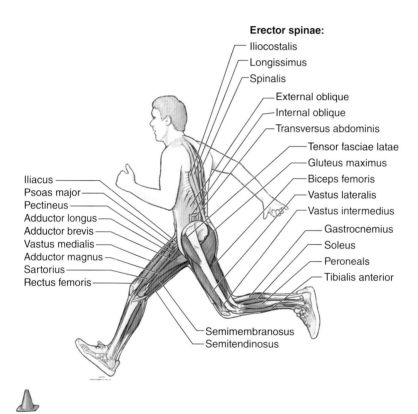

External oblique
Internal oblique
Transversus abdominis
Tensor fasciae latae
Gluteus maximus
Biceps femoris
Vastus lateralis
Vastus intermedius
Gastrocnemius
Soleus
Peroneals
Tibialis anterior

Iliacus
Psoas major
Pectineus
Adductor longus
Adductor brevis
Vastus medialis
Adductor magnus
Sartorius
Rectus femoris

Semimembranosus
Semitendinosus

Execution

1. Lie on the ground. Position can vary. Try beginning on your abdomen with your head at the starting line; on your abdomen with your feet at the starting line; on your abdomen, lying parallel to the starting line; on your back with your head at the starting line; on your back with your feet at the starting line; or on your back, lying parallel to the starting line.

2. On command, get up and sprint in the direction designed for the drill. Ways to get up can vary: Get up straight from your position on the ground and sprint in the designated direction, or roll over from your position on the ground, get up, and sprint.

Muscles Involved

Primary: Quadriceps (rectus femoris, vastus lateralis, vastus medius, vastus intermedius), hamstrings (semitendinosus, semimembranosus, biceps femoris), gluteus maximus, gastrocnemius, soleus, tibialis posterior, peroneals, tibialis anterior, psoas major, iliacus, tensor fasciae latae, sartorius, adductor longus, adductor brevis, adductor magnus, pectineus

Secondary: Internal oblique, external oblique, transversus abdominis, erector spinae (iliocostalis, longissimus, spinalis)

HOCKEY FOCUS

Players are knocked down and fall constantly during the course of a game. Therefore, it is necessary to develop the ability to get up from whatever position you are in and get to top speed as quickly as possible so you can be involved in the play or get back into the play.

VARIATION

Ground Start Rapids

Perform the ground start drill, except sprint a designated distance and then immediately get down into the same starting position and get up to sprint back to the starting line. You could also change the starting position. A coach or partner could call out the new position midrun or before the start of the repetition.

AGILITY

Agility is the ability of the body to change position rapidly in a coordinated, quick, and balanced way. In hockey, improved agility allows you to respond more quickly and efficiently to the frantic pace of the game. If you can reposition your body in the most efficient way, you will have the advantage when the puck changes direction or when you react to other players.

Agility improves when speed, balance, coordination, and strength are optimized and used together. Agility involves anticipation of the next activity and your ability to position your body in space to best accomplish that activity quickly and efficiently. Controlling the center of gravity is critical to agility in nearly every aspect of hockey. All of your muscle groups, both small and large, are critical to developing agility.

PRO AGILITY

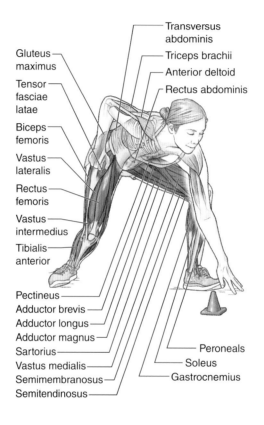

Transversus
abdominis

Gluteus
maximus

Triceps brachii

Anterior deltoid

Tensor
fasciae
latae

Rectus abdominis

Biceps
femoris

Vastus
lateralis

Rectus
femoris

Vastus
intermedius

Tibialis
anterior

Pectineus
Adductor brevis
Adductor longus
Adductor magnus
Sartorius
Vastus medialis
Semimembranosus
Semitendinosus

Peroneals
Soleus
Gastrocnemius

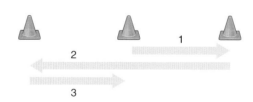

Execution

1. Straddle a 10-yard (9 m) midline with one hand on the ground.
2. Sprint to the right line 5 yards (4.6 m) away.
3. Touch the line with the right hand.
4. Immediately change direction and sprint through the start to the far line 10 yards away.
5. Touch that line with the left hand.
6. Sprint back through the starting line.
7. Repeat, switching the lead direction.

Muscles Involved

Primary: Quadriceps (rectus femoris, vastus lateralis, vastus medius, vastus intermedius), hamstrings (semitendinosus, semimembranosus, biceps femoris), gluteus maximus, gastrocnemius, soleus, tibialis posterior, peroneals, tibialis anterior, iliopsoas, tensor fasciae latae, sartorius, adductor longus, adductor brevis, adductor magnus, pectineus

Secondary: Rectus abdominis, transversus abdominis, anterior deltoid, triceps brachii

HOCKEY FOCUS

The ability to stop and change direction in small spaces and reaccelerate quickly will help you beat the competitor to the puck. This drill focuses on a linear change of direction that emphasizes staying low and exploding out of the stops and starts. It will help you learn to balance and transfer your body weight in a ballistic fashion, which will enhance speed and acceleration and deceleration.

AGILITY

DIAGONAL FOUR CONES

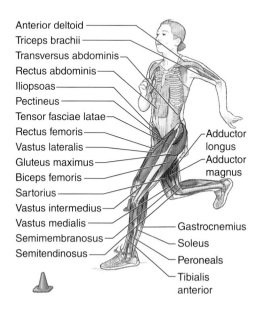

Anterior deltoid
Triceps brachii
Transversus abdominis
Rectus abdominis
Iliopsoas
Pectineus
Tensor fasciae latae
Rectus femoris
Vastus lateralis
Gluteus maximus
Biceps femoris
Sartorius
Vastus intermedius
Vastus medialis
Semimembranosus
Semitendinosus

Adductor longus
Adductor magnus
Gastrocnemius
Soleus
Peroneals
Tibialis anterior

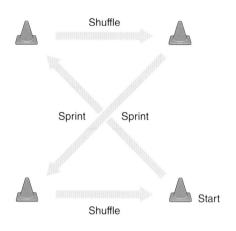

Shuffle

Sprint   Sprint

Shuffle   Start

Execution

1. Set out four cones to create a square with sides 10-yards (9 m) long. (The square could be smaller for a quicker change-of-direction drill.)
2. Start at one corner and sprint diagonally to the opposite corner.
3. Shuffle across the top of the box.
4. Pivot in toward the box and sprint diagonally to the cone opposite the starting cone.
5. Shuffle across to the start.
6. Repeat, but this time pivot away from the box at the top of the square before sprinting diagonally to the lower cone opposite the starting cone.

Muscles Involved

Primary: Quadriceps (rectus femoris, vastus lateralis, vastus medius, vastus intermedius), hamstrings (semitendinosus, semimembranosus, biceps femoris), gluteus maximus, gastrocnemius, soleus, tibialis posterior, peroneals, tibialis anterior, iliopsoas, tensor fasciae latae, sartorius, adductor longus, adductor brevis, adductor magnus, pectineus

Secondary: Rectus abdominis, transversus abdominis, anterior deltoid, triceps brachii

HOCKEY FOCUS

This is a small-space, multidirectional pattern drill as well as a footwork drill. The ability to move one's feet and pivot quickly on the ice to accelerate or change direction is vital. This drill also emphasizes lateral movement, which develops a low center of gravity in conjunction with hip movement to create speed coming out of the turns. This is a great drill for goalies who need to come out to the corner of the crease and move laterally to change their angle so they can see and then stop a puck. It is also important for their post-to-post lateral push-offs.

VARIATION

Diagonal Crossover

Perform the drill using crossover steps instead of shuffling or a combination of both types of footwork.

W DRILL

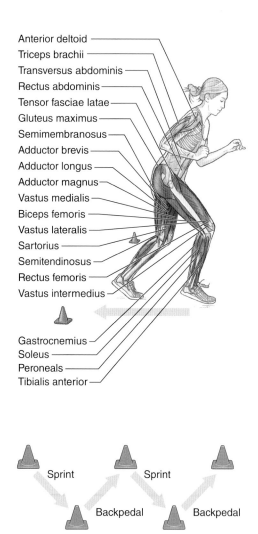

Anterior deltoid
Triceps brachii
Transversus abdominis
Rectus abdominis
Tensor fasciae latae
Gluteus maximus
Semimembranosus
Adductor brevis
Adductor longus
Adductor magnus
Vastus medialis
Biceps femoris
Vastus lateralis
Sartorius
Semitendinosus
Rectus femoris
Vastus intermedius

Gastrocnemius
Soleus
Peroneals
Tibialis anterior

Sprint   Sprint

Backpedal   Backpedal

Execution

1. Set out 10 cones 3 yards (2.7 m) apart from each other in a diagonal pattern.
2. Starting at the first cone, sprint diagonally to the next cone.
3. Once at that cone, immediately backpedal diagonally to the next cone. You can make a sharp change of direction or round the tops and bottoms of the cones.
4. Continue in this manner for all cones.
5. Repeat immediately, going back to the start.

Muscles Involved

Primary: Quadriceps (rectus femoris, vastus lateralis, vastus medius, vastus intermedius), hamstrings (semitendinosus, semimembranosus, biceps femoris), gluteus maximus, gastrocnemius, soleus, tibialis posterior, peroneals, tibialis anterior, iliopsoas, tensor fasciae latae, sartorius, adductor longus, adductor brevis, adductor magnus, pectineus

Secondary: Rectus abdominis, transversus abdominis, anterior deltoid, triceps brachii

HOCKEY FOCUS

This drill helps you maintain a low center of gravity while moving your feet in and out of the cones as quickly as possible. Because not all movement on the ice is forward, it is necessary to learn to move the feet and transition momentum backward. Although this backpedal pattern is not replicated when skating on the ice, the ability to rapidly accelerate and decelerate in both the forward and backward direction is.

AGILITY

CHUTE

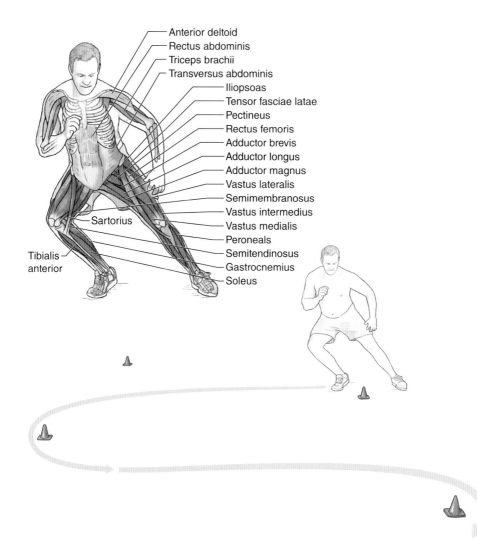

Anterior deltoid
Rectus abdominis
Triceps brachii
Transversus abdominis
Iliopsoas
Tensor fasciae latae
Pectineus
Rectus femoris
Adductor brevis
Adductor longus
Adductor magnus
Vastus lateralis
Semimembranosus
Vastus intermedius
Vastus medialis
Peroneals
Semitendinosus
Gastrocnemius
Soleus

Sartorius

Tibialis
anterior

Execution

1. Set out 10 cones 3 yards (2.7 m) apart from each other in a diagonal pattern.
2. Starting at the first cone, sprint diagonally to the next cone, plant on the outside foot, and reaccelerate to the next cone.
3. You can go around the outside of the cone and also backward.
4. Continue in this manner until the end of the run.

Muscles Involved

Primary: Quadriceps (rectus femoris, vastus lateralis, vastus medius, vastus intermedius), hamstrings (semitendinosus, semimembranosus, biceps femoris), gluteus maximus, gastrocnemius, soleus, tibialis posterior, peroneals, tibialis anterior, iliopsoas, tensor fasciae latae, sartorius, adductor longus, adductor brevis, adductor magnus, pectineus

Secondary: Rectus abdominis, transversus abdominis, anterior deltoid, triceps brachii

HOCKEY FOCUS

This drill keeps the feet moving under you as quickly as possible. In addition, it develops quick lateral push-off in both directions when you need to rapidly change direction in small spaces. The development of this lateral push is important on the ice when you want to quickly change pace and direction to avoid a defender and for goalies to be able to push to the many angles of the crease.

SPRINT AGILITY

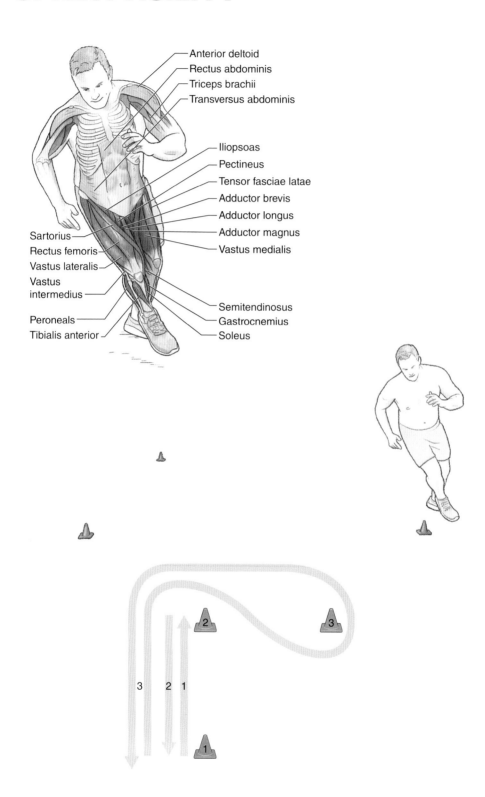

Anterior deltoid
Rectus abdominis
Triceps brachii
Transversus abdominis

Iliopsoas
Pectineus
Tensor fasciae latae
Adductor brevis
Adductor longus
Adductor magnus
Vastus medialis

Sartorius
Rectus femoris
Vastus lateralis
Vastus intermedius

Peroneals
Tibialis anterior

Semitendinosus
Gastrocnemius
Soleus

Execution

1. Set up three cones 5 yards (4.6 m) apart in an upside-down L shape.
2. Starting at one end of the L, sprint straight ahead to cone 2 and touch the line.
3. Sprint back to the starting cone and touch the line.
4. Sprint up and around cone 2 and on the inside of cone 3.
5. Continue sprinting around the outside of cone 2 and through the starting line.
6. Move cone 1 to the other side to face cone 3 and repeat.

Muscles Involved

Primary: Quadriceps (rectus femoris, vastus lateralis, vastus medius, vastus intermedius), hamstrings (semitendinosus, semimembranosus, biceps femoris), gluteus maximus, gastrocnemius, soleus, tibialis posterior, peroneals, tibialis anterior, iliopsoas, tensor fasciae latae, sartorius, adductor longus, adductor brevis, adductor magnus, pectineus

Secondary: Rectus abdominis, transversus abdominis, anterior deltoid, triceps brachii

HOCKEY FOCUS

The drill requires multiple changes of direction, quick feet, and the ability to lower the center of gravity to round the turn and reaccelerate. It is important to emphasize speed out of the turns in all facets of the drill. This is seen on the ice all the time, when a player turns to backcheck or elude another player. This ability to anticipate and respond to stimulus to change direction but also reaccelerate is vital in the game.

FIGURE-8 DRILL

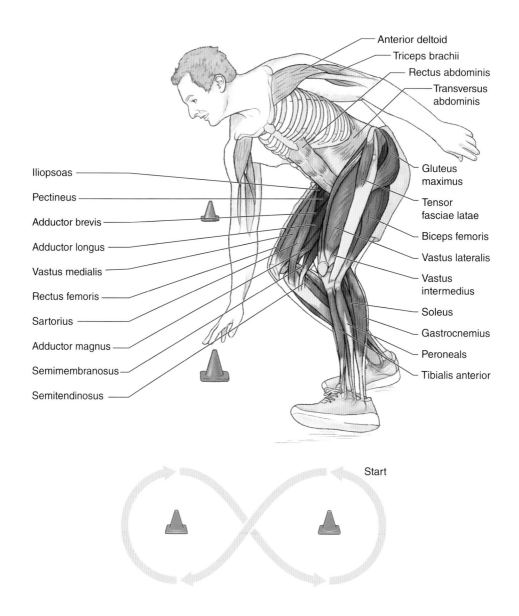

Anterior deltoid
Triceps brachii
Rectus abdominis
Transversus abdominis
Gluteus maximus
Tensor fasciae latae
Biceps femoris
Vastus lateralis
Vastus intermedius
Soleus
Gastrocnemius
Peroneals
Tibialis anterior

Iliopsoas
Pectineus
Adductor brevis
Adductor longus
Vastus medialis
Rectus femoris
Sartorius
Adductor magnus
Semimembranosus
Semitendinosus

Start

Execution

1. Set up two cones 10 yards (9 m) apart.
2. Run in a figure-8 pattern around the cones.
3. Touch each cone and stay low while making the turns.
4. Repeat for the allotted number of turns and repetitions.

Muscles Involved

Primary: Quadriceps (rectus femoris, vastus lateralis, vastus medius, vastus intermedius), hamstrings (semitendinosus, semimembranosus, biceps femoris), gluteus maximus, gastrocnemius, soleus, tibialis posterior, peroneals, tibialis anterior, iliopsoas, tensor fasciae latae, sartorius, adductor longus, adductor brevis, adductor magnus, pectineus

Secondary: Rectus abdominis, transversus abdominis, anterior deltoid, triceps brachii

HOCKEY FOCUS

Because players must turn frequently to avoid another player or to get better position on the ice in relation to the puck or the play, staying low while turning is important for skating efficiency. Success comes with the ability to control the body's center of gravity and still maintain high levels of speed. This drill emphasizes quick changes in speed and direction while keeping a low base and maintaining and increasing speed out of the turns.

VARIATION

Shuffle or Backpedal Figure 8

This drill can be performed using backpedal or shuffle footwork.

AGILITY

T TEST

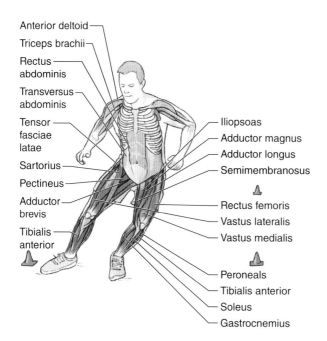

Anterior deltoid
Triceps brachii
Rectus abdominis
Transversus abdominis
Tensor fasciae latae
Sartorius
Pectineus
Adductor brevis
Tibialis anterior

Iliopsoas
Adductor magnus
Adductor longus
Semimembranosus
Rectus femoris
Vastus lateralis
Vastus medialis
Peroneals
Tibialis anterior
Soleus
Gastrocnemius

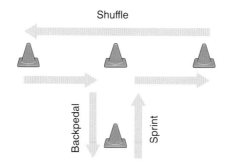

Shuffle

Backpedal

Sprint

Execution

1. Set up four cones in a T configuration. Three cones 5 yards (4.6 m) apart make up the top of the T. Set the fourth cone 5 yards (4.6 m) from the middle cone to create the bottom of the T.
2. Start at the bottom of the T and run to the middle cone.
3. Shuffle right to the next cone.
4. Shuffle all the way across to the far cone at the top of the T.
5. Shuffle back to the middle cone.
6. Run backward through the starting cone.

Muscles Involved

Primary: Quadriceps (rectus femoris, vastus lateralis, vastus medius, vastus intermedius), hamstrings (semitendinosus, semimembranosus, biceps femoris), gluteus maximus, gastrocnemius, soleus, tibialis posterior, peroneals, tibialis anterior, iliopsoas, tensor fasciae latae, sartorius, adductor longus, adductor brevis, adductor magnus, pectineus

Secondary: Rectus abdominis, transversus abdominis, anterior deltoid, triceps brachii

HOCKEY FOCUS

Reading and responding to the play on the ice demands the ability to visually anticipate what is happening and then act quickly and appropriately to the information. This drill emphasizes forward, lateral, and backward speed, but requires you to change direction sharply and with speed by anticipating what to do next at each cone.

ILLINOIS AGILITY

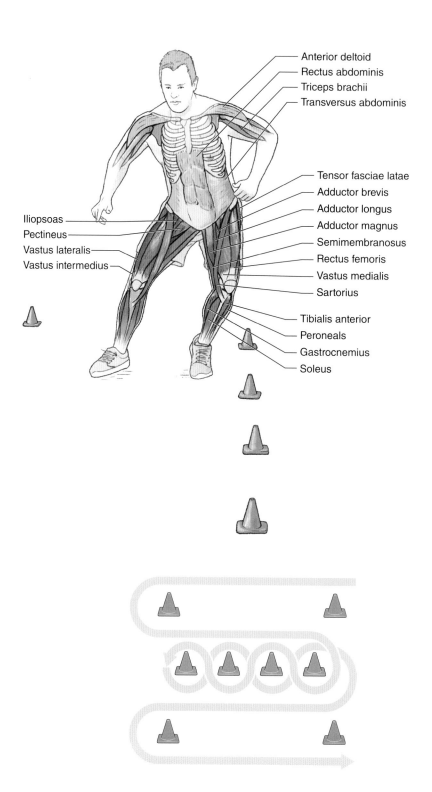

Anterior deltoid
Rectus abdominis
Triceps brachii
Transversus abdominis

Tensor fasciae latae
Adductor brevis
Adductor longus
Adductor magnus
Semimembranosus
Rectus femoris
Vastus medialis
Sartorius

Tibialis anterior
Peroneals
Gastrocnemius
Soleus

Iliopsoas
Pectineus
Vastus lateralis
Vastus intermedius

Execution

1. Set up eight cones in the pattern shown. The top cones are 10 yards (9 m) apart from each other. The bottom cones are 10 yards apart from each other and from the top cones. The middle cones are 2 yards apart (1.8 m) from each other and set up about halfway between the top and bottom cones.
2. Start at one of the top cones and sprint 10 yards to the second top cone.
3. Run around the cone and over to the far middle cone. Run around each middle cone down the line and back.
4. After running around the middle cones, run to the far bottom cone and finish by running to the far bottom cone.

Muscles Involved

Primary: Quadriceps (rectus femoris, vastus lateralis, vastus medius, vastus intermedius), hamstrings (semitendinosus, semimembranosus, biceps femoris), gluteus maximus, gastrocnemius, soleus, tibialis posterior, peroneals, tibialis anterior, iliopsoas, tensor fasciae latae, sartorius, adductor longus, adductor brevis, adductor magnus, pectineus

Secondary: Rectus abdominis, transversus abdominis, anterior deltoid, triceps brachii

HOCKEY FOCUS

It is necessary to be able to move and pivot the hips in relation to the feet quickly in and out of tight spaces. For puck handling, it is important for the feet and hips to move in and out of traffic by controlling the lower half. This drill will improve your ability to do this while creating speed and positioning the lower body so it can turn sharply and maximize the use of the skates' edges.

CROSSOVER BACK STEP ACCELERATION

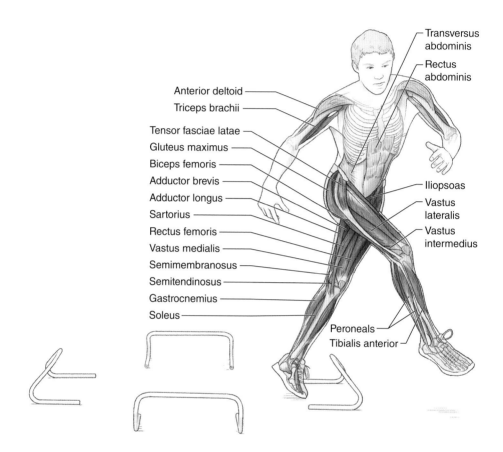

Transversus abdominis

Rectus abdominis

Anterior deltoid

Triceps brachii

Tensor fasciae latae

Gluteus maximus

Biceps femoris

Adductor brevis

Adductor longus

Sartorius

Rectus femoris

Vastus medialis

Semimembranosus

Semitendinosus

Gastrocnemius

Soleus

Iliopsoas

Vastus lateralis

Vastus intermedius

Peroneals

Tibialis anterior

Execution

1. Set up minihurdles in a box pattern; hurdles are 4 feet (1.2 m) apart from each other.
2. Starting on one side of the box, cross over the outside foot (left) into the box.
3. Step the other foot (right) into the box.
4. Cross over (left) out of the box.
5. Step out of the box with the right foot, plant on that foot, and then cross over with that foot into the box.

6. Step the left foot into the box.

7. Step the right foot back over the back of the box.

8. Step the left foot back over the back of the box, plant, and then accelerate to run forward through the box and out.

9. Repeat with the other foot leading.

Muscles Involved

Primary: Quadriceps (rectus femoris, vastus lateralis, vastus medius, vastus intermedius), hamstrings (semitendinosus, semimembranosus, biceps femoris), gluteus maximus, gastrocnemius, soleus, tibialis posterior, peroneals, tibialis anterior, iliopsoas, tensor fasciae latae, sartorius, adductor longus, adductor brevis, adductor magnus, pectineus

Secondary: Rectus abdominis, transversus abdominis, anterior deltoid, triceps brachii

HOCKEY FOCUS

The speed and power out of each crossover step is important for moving laterally, turning, and accelerating both forward and backward. These movements allow you to avoid potential defenders or to change position to defend the puck and player. The ability to gather the feet under the center of gravity to change direction while driving the foot into the ground allows you to develop the force that propels the body laterally.

HURDLE HOP CIRCLE

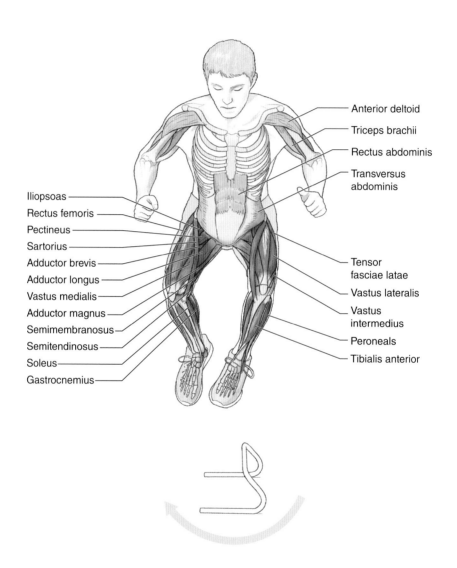

Anterior deltoid

Triceps brachii

Rectus abdominis

Transversus abdominis

Iliopsoas

Rectus femoris

Pectineus

Sartorius

Adductor brevis

Adductor longus

Vastus medialis

Adductor magnus

Semimembranosus

Semitendinosus

Soleus

Gastrocnemius

Tensor fasciae latae

Vastus lateralis

Vastus intermedius

Peroneals

Tibialis anterior

Execution

1. Stand on one side of a 6- to 12-inch (15-30 cm) hurdle and perform a double-footed lateral jump over it.
2. After completing the jump, run around the hurdle. Always face one direction. Keep a low center of gravity until you reach the opposite side of the hurdle.
3. Perform another jump back to the starting position.
4. Repeat this pattern for the allotted number of repetitions per set.

Muscles Involved

Primary: Quadriceps (rectus femoris, vastus lateralis, vastus medius, vastus intermedius), hamstrings (semitendinosus, semimembranosus, biceps femoris), gluteus maximus, gastrocnemius, soleus, tibialis posterior, peroneals, tibialis anterior, iliopsoas, tensor fasciae latae, sartorius, adductor longus, adductor brevis, adductor magnus, pectineus

Secondary: Rectus abdominis, transversus abdominis, anterior deltoid, triceps brachii

HOCKEY FOCUS

Plyometrics performed near the ground are necessary for developing a quick response off the ground before a movement. This is necessary for developing single-leg power and quickness as well as to learn to control the body in space. During a game, the feet are not always planted firmly on the ice while skating or changing direction. A quick response once the feet hit the ice when hopping over boards, evading, jumping, circling, and carving is vital. These movements use the ability to perform small-space change of directions.

VARIATIONS

Two-Hurdle Hop

Set up two hurdles 3 feet (1 m) apart. Jump laterally over one hurdle and then the other. After completing the jumps, run around both hurdles.

Single-Leg Lateral Hop

Hop over the hurdle on one leg, and then perform the run.

Figure 8

Set up two hurdles 3 feet (1 m) apart. Start on one side of the first hurdle. Hop into the center. Run over the top of the second hurdle to get to the side of it that is farthest away from the first hurdle. Hop over the second hurdle into the center of the two hurdles again. Run behind the first hurdle to get to the side of it. Repeat for the allotted number of repetitions.

MOBILITY

Achieving maximum mobility in hockey allows peak performance and can help prevent injury. Many hockey-specific examples of mobility exist, but one of the easiest to understand is performing the slapshot. Opening up during the windup before the shot requires mobilization of the entire back and the shoulders and hips. The athlete who has more mobility and can open up more will have more of an arc through which to accelerate. This allows more stick speed at the time of impact, which will propel the puck faster. Mobility in goalies is also an absolute necessity for performing at a high level.

Injury prevention is another benefit of mobility. Absorbing impact and the forces applied during contact and collision is a constant part of the game. At the end of each joint's arc of motion, the tissues of the joint absorb all of the energy, which can result in damage to those tissues. Improving your mobility improves your game and can help you avoid injury.

FOOT MASSAGE WITH BALL

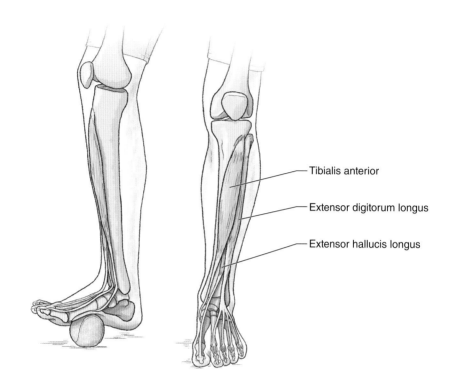

Tibialis anterior

Extensor digitorum longus

Extensor hallucis longus

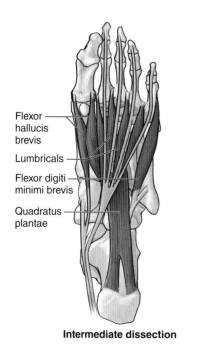

Flexor hallucis brevis

Lumbricals

Flexor digiti minimi brevis

Quadratus plantae

Intermediate dissection

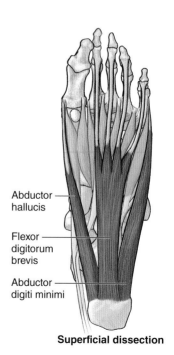

Abductor hallucis

Flexor digitorum brevis

Abductor digiti minimi

Superficial dissection

Execution

1. You can either stand or sit for this drill.
2. Place a lacrosse or golf ball under one foot.
3. Move the ball in a circle with the foot. Focus on sensitive spots on the base of the foot.
4. Continue rolling for the allotted time and then switch feet.

Muscles Involved

Primary: Flexor digitorum brevis, flexor hallucis brevis, adductor hallucis, abductor digiti minimi

Secondary: Tibialis anterior, extensor digitorum longus, extensor hallucis longus

HOCKEY FOCUS

The foot is trapped in a restricted skating boot during the season, leading to restriction of the foot muscles. This exercise restores normal tissue elasticity, improves blood flow to the tissue, and readies the muscles and tendons of the foot and ankle for activity. Performing this drill every day before putting on skates will improve circulation and range of motion.

WALL ANKLE FLEXION

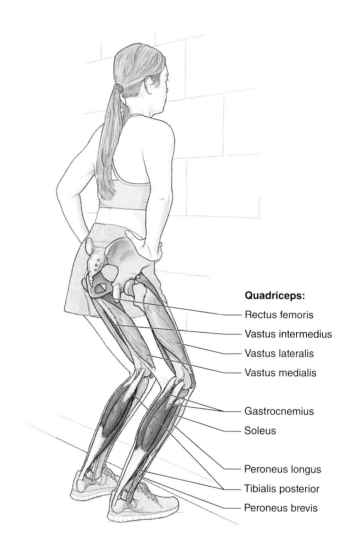

Quadriceps:
Rectus femoris
Vastus intermedius
Vastus lateralis
Vastus medialis

Gastrocnemius
Soleus

Peroneus longus
Tibialis posterior
Peroneus brevis

Execution

1. Stand facing a wall. The legs are shoulder-width apart and the toes a few inches from the wall.
2. Keep the heels flat and bend the knees until they touch the wall and hold for a two count.
3. Return to the starting position.
4. Perform the allotted number of repetitions.

Muscles Involved

Primary: Gastrocnemius, soleus, tibialis posterior

Secondary: Peroneus longus, peroneus brevis, quadriceps (rectus femoris, vastus lateralis, vastus medialis, vastus intermedius)

HOCKEY FOCUS

Range of motion in the ankle contributes to better contact between the skate and the entire foot throughout the stride, which improves skating efficiency. In addition, the ability to achieve high degrees of ankle flexion while in the skate allows you to carve deeper into the ice with a shorter turning radius.

STANDING-T SPINE ROTATION

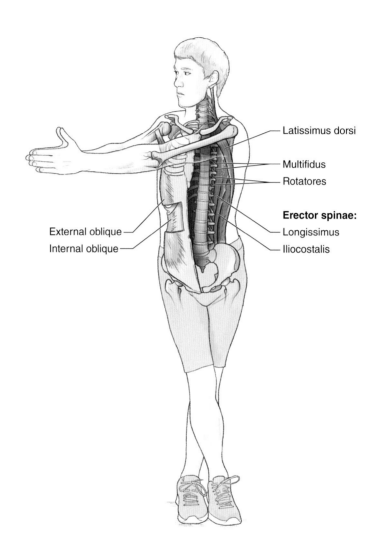

Latissimus dorsi

Multifidus

Rotatores

Erector spinae:

Longissimus

Iliocostalis

External oblique

Internal oblique

Execution

1. Stand tall. Cross one foot over the other so the feet are together, toes aligned, and legs straight.
2. Raise the arms straight in front at shoulder height with the palms together.
3. With arms straight, rotate the torso toward the side of the leg that is crossed over. For example, if the right foot is crossed over the left foot, turn the torso to the right.
4. Return to the starting position.
5. Repeat for the allotted number of repetitions, and then switch to the other side.

Muscles Involved

Primary: Latissimus dorsi, multifidus, rotatores, erector spinae (iliocostalis, longissimus, spinalis)

Secondary: External oblique, internal oblique

HOCKEY FOCUS

Spinal rotational mobility is critical while shooting and while crossing over and skating backward. Goalies depend on spinal rotational mobility when the puck is deep in the defensive zone or behind the goal or when the goalie has to reach behind himself to make a save on the opposite side of the net.

VARIATION

Quadruped T-Spine Rotation

Assume an all-fours position on hands and knees. Raise one hand high behind the back or place it on the back of the head. Rotate the torso to open up to the side of the raised hand. Rotate the torso the other way toward the elbow of the hand that is still on the ground. Perform the allotted number of repetitions and then switch sides.

GIANT LEG CIRCLES

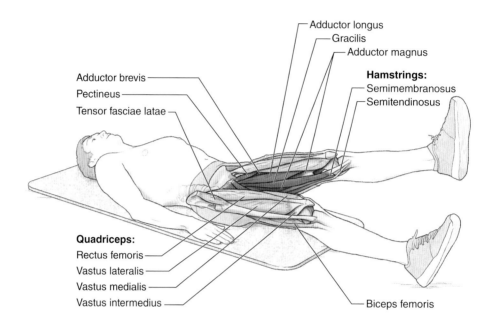

Adductor longus

Gracilis

Adductor magnus

Hamstrings:
Semimembranosus
Semitendinosus

Adductor brevis

Pectineus

Tensor fasciae latae

Quadriceps:
Rectus femoris
Vastus lateralis
Vastus medialis
Vastus intermedius

Biceps femoris

Execution

1. Lie faceup on the floor.
2. Keeping both legs straight, lift one and point the toes toward the ceiling.
3. With that leg, make giant circles above the body, always coming above hip height on each circle.
4. Make circles both clockwise and counterclockwise for the allotted number of repetitions and then perform the drill with the other leg.

Muscles Involved

Primary: Adductor magnus, adductor longus, adductor brevis, pectineus, gracilis

Secondary: Hamstrings (semitendinosus, semimembranosus, biceps femoris), tensor fasciae latae, quadriceps (rectus femoris, vastus lateralis, vastus medialis, vastus intermedius)

HOCKEY FOCUS

Hip mobility is required in all aspects of skating and shooting. Goalies require hip mobility to get into a butterfly position, to perform kick saves, and to push from post to post.

KNEE GRAB

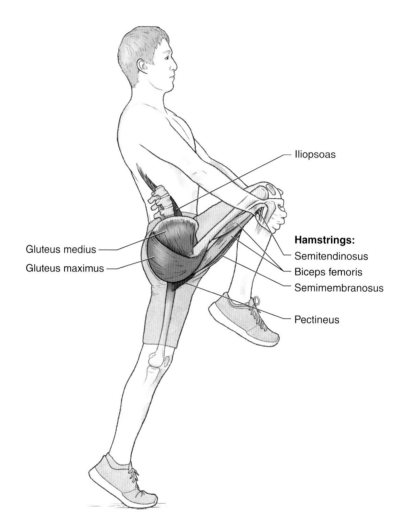

Iliopsoas

Gluteus medius

Gluteus maximus

Hamstrings:
Semitendinosus
Biceps femoris
Semimembranosus

Pectineus

Walking knee grab.

Execution

1. Players can perform the knee grab while lying faceup on the ground, while standing, and while walking.
2. Begin with both legs straight.
3. Bring one knee up to the chest and hug it to the body.
4. If standing or walking, lift the heel of the standing leg off the ground as you pull the knee to the chest.
5. Return the leg to the starting position and lift the opposite leg.
6. Repeat for the allotted number of repetitions or for distance if walking.

Muscles Involved

Primary (knee pulled into chest): Gluteus maximus, gluteus medius

Secondary (knee pulled into chest): Hamstrings (semitendinosus, semimembranosus, biceps femoris)

Primary (standing leg): Iliopsoas, pectineus

HOCKEY FOCUS

Hip flexibility is crucial for all power-skating activities. When a hockey player needs to accelerate quickly or turn sharply, range of motion in the hips is critical.

MOBILITY

ANKLE GRAB

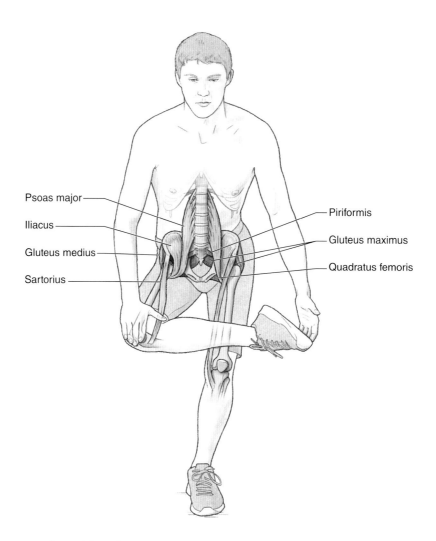

Psoas major
Iliacus
Gluteus medius
Sartorius

Piriformis
Gluteus maximus
Quadratus femoris

Standing ankle grab.

Execution

1. Players can perform the ankle grab while lying faceup, while standing, or while walking.
2. Begin with both legs straight.
3. Bring one foot up to the knee of the standing leg and then cross it over the leg.
4. Pull up on the toes and push down on the knee of the leg that is crossed over. At the same time, squat.
5. Return to standing and lower the leg. Repeat on the other side.
6. Repeat for the allotted number of repetitions or for distance if walking.

Muscles Involved

Primary: Gluteus maximus, piriformis, quadratus femoris

Secondary: Gluteus medius, psoas major, iliacus, sartorius

HOCKEY FOCUS

Externally rotating the hip while skating creates the angle at which the blade cuts into the ice and allows the skater to generate depth and speed of the stride. Range of motion of the external rotators of the hips allows goalies to open up for pushes from post to post and to get up from the down position.

LATERAL LUNGE AND REACH

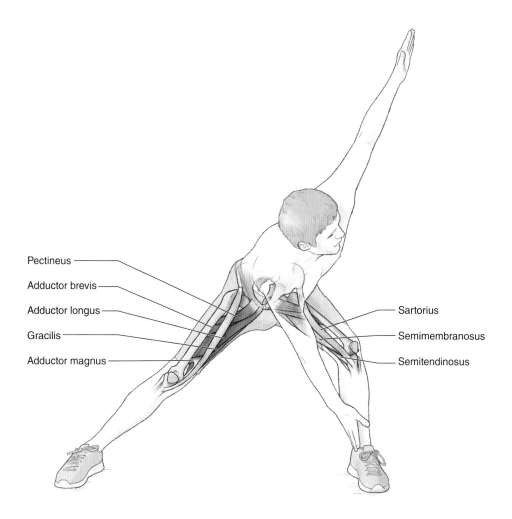

Pectineus

Adductor brevis

Adductor longus

Gracilis

Adductor magnus

Sartorius

Semimembranosus

Semitendinosus

Execution

1. Players can perform the lateral lunge and reach while standing still or while walking.
2. Stand with the feet wide apart.
3. Bend one knee to lower into a lateral lunge. The opposite leg is straight.
4. Keeping the arms straight, reach down with the hand on the side opposite the bent leg to the foot on the side of the bent leg.
5. At the same time, lift the hand on the side of the bent leg toward the ceiling, twisting at the waist.
6. Pause for one count, and then return to the standing position.
7. If performing with alternating walking for a specific distance, flip around and bend the other leg, performing the twist to the other side. Continue in the alternating walking fashion for the allotted distance. Perform the required number of repetitions per side if standing still.

Muscles Involved

Primary: Adductor magnus, adductor longus, adductor brevis, pectineus, gracilis

Secondary: Semitendinosus, semimembranosus, sartorius

HOCKEY FOCUS

Lateral lunging movements improve hip flexion and extension, lumbar and thoracic spine extension, and shoulder forward flexion in addition to activating the quadriceps and core muscles. The adductor group tends to shorten because of skating mechanics. It is necessary to keep these muscles long so the skating motion does not become compromised.

VARIATION

Lateral Lunge Twisting Reach

Perform a lateral lunge to one side. Turn the torso toward the bent knee to go into a deep forward lunge. With the arm on the side of the forward leg, reach overhead while twisting the torso toward the front knee.

REACHING SINGLE-LEG HAM AND QUAD

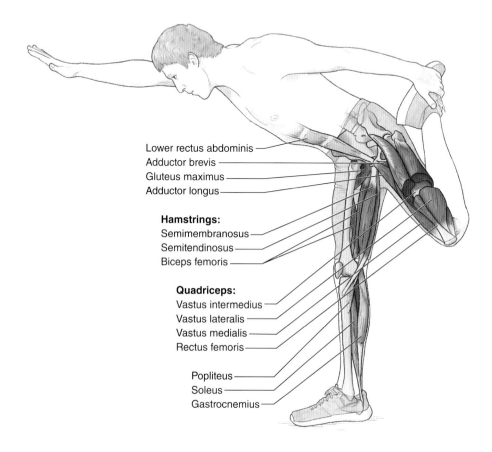

Lower rectus abdominis
Adductor brevis
Gluteus maximus
Adductor longus

Hamstrings:
Semimembranosus
Semitendinosus
Biceps femoris

Quadriceps:
Vastus intermedius
Vastus lateralis
Vastus medialis
Rectus femoris

Popliteus
Soleus
Gastrocnemius

Execution

1. Athletes can perform the reaching single-leg ham and quad while standing or walking.
2. Stand with both legs straight.
3. Grab the ankle of one leg behind the back with the hand on the same side.
4. At the same time, reach up and stretch the opposite arm towards the ceiling.
5. Bend forward at the waist while reaching with the arm and keeping the planted leg straight and the other leg bent behind you.
6. Stand up and repeat on the opposite side.
7. Continue for the allotted number of repetitions or for distance.

Muscles Involved

Primary (stance leg): Hamstrings (semitendinosus, semimembranosus, biceps femoris), gluteus maximus

Primary (bent leg): Quadriceps (rectus femoris, vastus lateralis, vastus medialis, vastus intermedius), adductor longus, adductor magnus, adductor brevis

Secondary (stance leg): Soleus, gastrocnemius, popliteus

Secondary (bent leg): Lower rectus abdominis

HOCKEY FOCUS

The ability to lengthen the entire kinetic chain in one movement is a positive for hockey players. This movement alleviates some of the tightness that players experience, especially in the quadriceps, and lengthens the entire pelvis.

SPIDERMAN WITH INTERNAL ROTATION

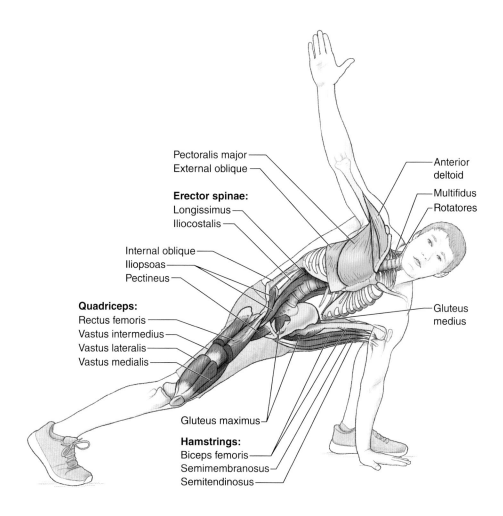

Pectoralis major
External oblique

Anterior deltoid

Multifidus
Rotatores

Erector spinae:
Longissimus
Iliocostalis

Internal oblique
Iliopsoas
Pectineus

Quadriceps:
Rectus femoris
Vastus intermedius
Vastus lateralis
Vastus medialis

Gluteus medius

Gluteus maximus

Hamstrings:
Biceps femoris
Semimembranosus
Semitendinosus

Execution

1. Players can perform the spiderman with internal rotation while stationary or while moving forward.
2. Begin on hands and knees.
3. Move one leg forward, and straighten the back leg. You will end up in an exaggerated lunge position with the back knee off the ground.
4. Bring the same-side elbow toward the front leg and place the hand on the ground beside the foot.
5. At the same time, reach toward the ceiling with the opposite arm and twist the torso away from the front leg.
6. Lower the arm and place the hand on the ground. Move the opposite leg forward and repeat on the other side.
7. Continue for the allotted number of repetitions or specified distance.

Muscles Involved

Primary (front leg): Gluteus maximus, gluteus medius, hamstrings (semitendinosus, semimembranosus, biceps femoris)

Primary (back leg): Iliopsoas, pectineus, quadriceps (rectus femoris, vastus lateralis, vastus medialis, vastus intermedius)

Secondary: Multifidus, rotatores, erector spinae (iliocostalis, longissimus, spinalis), pectoralis major, anterior deltoid, external oblique, internal oblique

HOCKEY FOCUS

The spiderman with internal rotation puts the body through a range of motion that prepares it for the forces that are generated in the same pattern as the stride and shot. For that reason, use this drill to prepare the body for subsequent low-skating and shooting drills.

VARIATION

Spiderman With External Rotation

Perform the same way as the spiderman with internal rotation, except touch the ground with the opposite side hand next to the front foot, and reach up with the same-side arm, twisting the torso toward the front leg.

129

TOE TOUCH ALTERNATING REACH TO OVERHEAD SQUAT

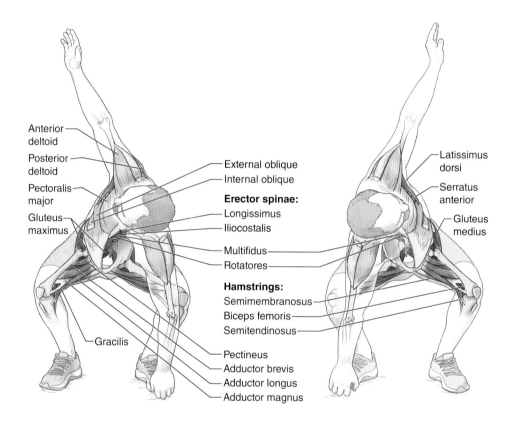

Anterior deltoid

Posterior deltoid

Pectoralis major

Gluteus maximus

Gracilis

External oblique

Internal oblique

Erector spinae:

Longissimus

Iliocostalis

Multifidus

Rotatores

Hamstrings:

Semimembranosus

Biceps femoris

Semitendinosus

Pectineus

Adductor brevis

Adductor longus

Adductor magnus

Latissimus dorsi

Serratus anterior

Gluteus medius

Execution

1. Stand with feet wider than shoulder width and legs straight. Reach up to the ceiling and lean back.
2. Let the torso fall forward, bowing at the waist and keeping the legs straight.
3. Grab the toes with the hands and squat down.
4. Reach one arm straight overhead and back by twisting the torso toward the arm that is reaching overhead.
5. Lower that hand and grab the same-side foot. Raise the other arm up and back, twisting at the torso.
6. Bring both arms straight overhead and stand up.
7. Repeat for the allotted number of repetitions.

Muscles Involved

Primary: Gluteus maximus, gluteus medius, hamstrings (semitendinosus, semimembranosus, biceps femoris), adductor magnus, adductor longus, adductor brevis, pectineus, gracilis

Secondary: Multifidus, rotatores, erector spinae (iliocostalis, longissimus, spinalis), pectoralis major, anterior deltoid, posterior deltoid, external oblique, internal oblique, latissimus dorsi, serratus anterior

HOCKEY FOCUS

This total-body exercise targets all of the aspects of mobility and flexibility required by hockey players. It provides motion in the hips and upper body, which is important for staying low in position to skate, take or give a hit, and shoot. For goalies, it opens the shoulders to make blocker and glove saves while staying in the low athletic position.

ROCKING HIP ROTATION

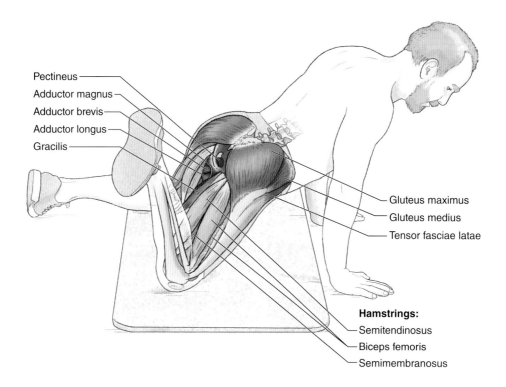

Pectineus
Adductor magnus
Adductor brevis
Adductor longus
Gracilis

Gluteus maximus
Gluteus medius
Tensor fasciae latae

Hamstrings:
Semitendinosus
Biceps femoris
Semimembranosus

Execution

1. Assume an all-fours position on the hands and knees.
2. Widen the knees to just outside shoulder-width apart.
3. Sit back on the heels, reaching out with the upper body.
4. Bring the hips forward and kick one foot up and out to the side.
5. Bring the foot back down and sit back on the heels.
6. Bring the hips forward and kick the other foot up and out to the side.
7. Repeat for the allotted number of repetitions per side.

Muscles Involved

Primary: Gluteus medius, gluteus minimus, tensor fasciae latae, adductor magnus, adductor longus, adductor brevis, pectineus, gracilis

Secondary: Hamstrings (semitendinosus, semimembranosus, biceps femoris)

HOCKEY FOCUS

This drill loosens the rotators of the hips in a rhythmic fashion. Because the hip rotators are instrumental in the ability to stay low while skating both backward and forward and in the ability of goalies to maintain a proper stance, it is vital to maintain mobility in this area of the lower limbs.

HIP CIRCLE

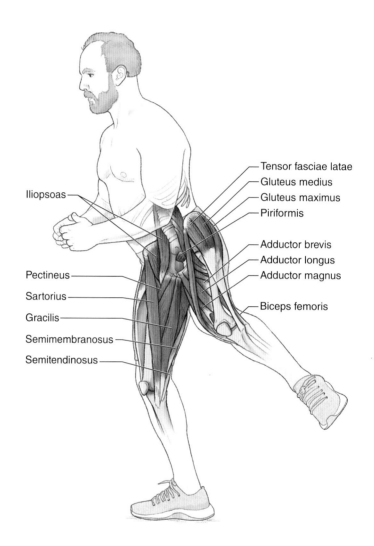

Iliopsoas

Pectineus

Sartorius

Gracilis

Semimembranosus

Semitendinosus

Tensor fasciae latae

Gluteus medius

Gluteus maximus

Piriformis

Adductor brevis

Adductor longus

Adductor magnus

Biceps femoris

Execution

1. Players can perform the hip circle forward or backward and while stationary or walking, jogging, or skipping.
2. Stand tall.
3. Bring one knee up and out to the side at hip level.
4. If walking backward, rotate the hip so the knee goes behind you. If walking forward, rotate the hip so the knee goes in front of you.
5. Bring the knee up and over the hip line and place the foot back on the ground.
6. Perform on the other side.

Muscles Involved

Primary: Gluteus maximus, gluteus medius, piriformis, tensor fasciae latae, adductor longus, adductor brevis, adductor magnus, pectineus, gracilis, sartorius

Secondary: Iliopsoas, hamstrings (semitendinosus, semimembranosus, biceps femoris)

HOCKEY FOCUS

This movement loosens the pelvis and hips, which is important for range of motion while skating and shooting.

HIGH-KNEE RUN

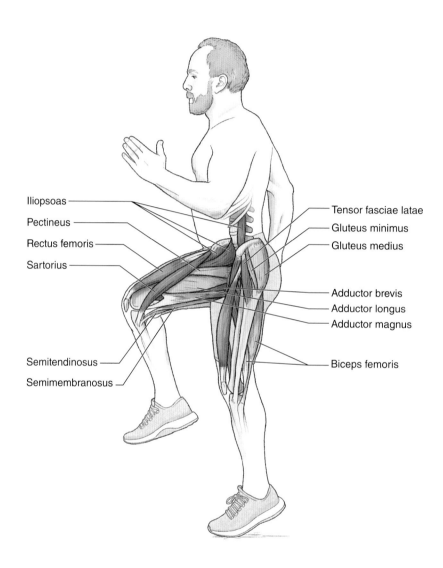

Iliopsoas

Pectineus

Rectus femoris

Sartorius

Semitendinosus

Semimembranosus

Tensor fasciae latae

Gluteus minimus

Gluteus medius

Adductor brevis

Adductor longus

Adductor magnus

Biceps femoris

Execution

1. Players can perform the high-knee run forward, backward, and laterally.
2. While moving rapidly in the designated direction, bring each knee up toward chest.
3. Bend the elbows to 90 degrees and swing the arms in opposition to the legs.
4. Land on the balls of the feet.
5. Perform for the allotted distance or time.

Muscles Involved

Primary: Iliopsoas, tensor fasciae latae, sartorius, rectus femoris

Secondary: Gluteus medius, gluteus minimus, adductor longus, adductor brevis, adductor magnus, pectineus, hamstrings (semitendinosus, semimembranosus, biceps femoris)

HOCKEY FOCUS

This is a general warm-up drill to work on hip flexion and elevate the heart rate in preparation for on-ice work. On the ice, it is important to draw the knee under the body on each successive stride, and this movement pattern mimics that positioning. The rapid turnover incurs more movement and range at the hips, which leads to a faster repositioning of the stride.

HIGH-KNEE SKIP

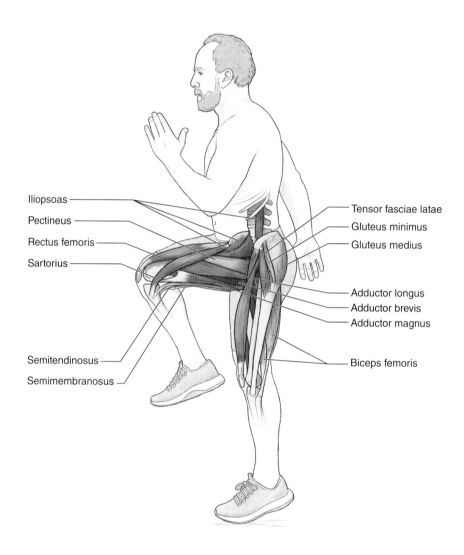

Iliopsoas

Pectineus

Rectus femoris

Sartorius

Semitendinosus

Semimembranosus

Tensor fasciae latae

Gluteus minimus

Gluteus medius

Adductor longus

Adductor brevis

Adductor magnus

Biceps femoris

Execution

1. Players can perform the high-knee skip forward, backward, or laterally.

2. While skipping rapidly in the designated direction, drive each knee up toward the chest. To skip, perform a small hop every time one foot touches the ground while moving forward, backward, or laterally, so that one foot touches the ground twice instead of once. During the small hop, the opposite knee comes to the chest.

3. Bend the elbows to 90 degrees, and swing the arms in opposition to the legs.

4. Land on the balls of the feet.

5. Perform for the allotted distance or time.

Muscles Involved

Primary: Iliopsoas, tensor fasciae latae, sartorius, rectus femoris, adductor longus, adductor magnus, adductor brevis

Secondary: Gluteus medius, gluteus minimus, hamstrings (semitendinosus, semimembranosus, biceps femoris), pectineus

HOCKEY FOCUS

This drill uses a rhythmic movement to improve the coordination and the range of motion used during a skating stride.

VARIATIONS

High-Knee Skip Crossover

Perform the high-knee skip, but cross the leg in front of the body while externally rotating the hip.

Russian March

Perform the high-knee skip while moving forward, but with a straight leg.

ANKLE HOP

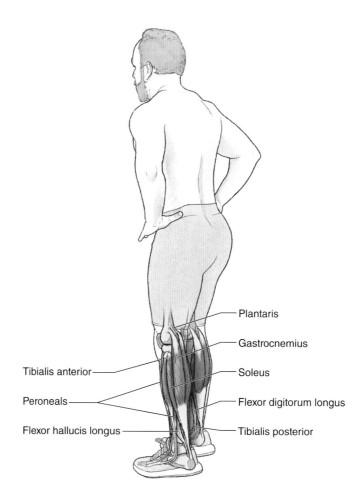

Tibialis anterior

Peroneals

Flexor hallucis longus

Plantaris

Gastrocnemius

Soleus

Flexor digitorum longus

Tibialis posterior

Execution

1. Players can perform the ankle hop while stationary or while moving forward or backward.

2. Keeping the legs straight or very slightly bent at the knees, hop vertically by pushing off the ground with the toes of both feet.

3. Hops should be performed using only the ankles. Avoid getting the quads involved by maintaining the knees in a fixed position.

4. Try to hop as high as possible while also pushing off the ground as quickly as possible.

5. Repeat for the allotted number of repetitions or for time.

Muscles Involved

Primary: Gastrocnemius, soleus, peroneals

Secondary: Tibialis posterior, tibialis anterior, flexor digitorum longus, flexor hallucis longus, plantaris

HOCKEY FOCUS

Enhancing ankle flexion and extension through this exercise benefits the skater most when making tight turns and pushing off to start skating.

LATERAL SHUFFLE WITH ARM SWING

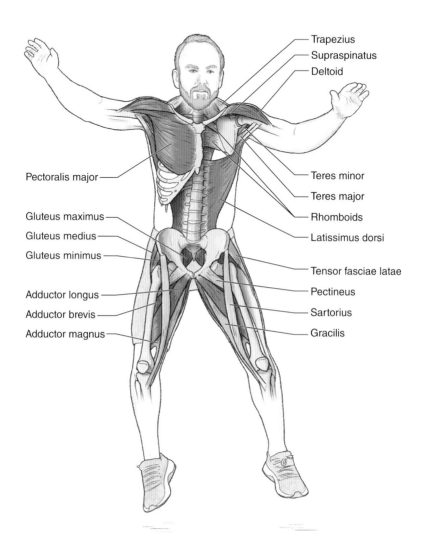

Trapezius

Supraspinatus

Deltoid

Pectoralis major

Teres minor

Teres major

Rhomboids

Latissimus dorsi

Gluteus maximus

Gluteus medius

Gluteus minimus

Tensor fasciae latae

Pectineus

Adductor longus

Sartorius

Adductor brevis

Gracilis

Adductor magnus

Execution

1. Start in an athletic position with the knees slightly bent and arms hanging down at the sides of the body.
2. Shuffle the feet with a wide base in one direction laterally.
3. At the same time, swing the arms across the body and then out to the sides as far as possible.
4. Perform for the allotted distance or time and then switch the direction of the shuffle.

Muscles Involved

Primary: Gluteus maximus, gluteus medius, gluteus minimus, adductor longus, adductor magnus, adductor brevis, deltoid, supraspinatus, latissimus dorsi, pectoralis major

Secondary: Pectineus, gracilis, sartorius, tensor fasciae latae, teres minor, teres major, trapezius, rhomboids

HOCKEY FOCUS

This motion opens up the lower half of the body in preparation for on-ice activity as well as warming up the upper body.

MOBILITY

CROSS OVER, CROSS BEHIND LATERAL LUNGE

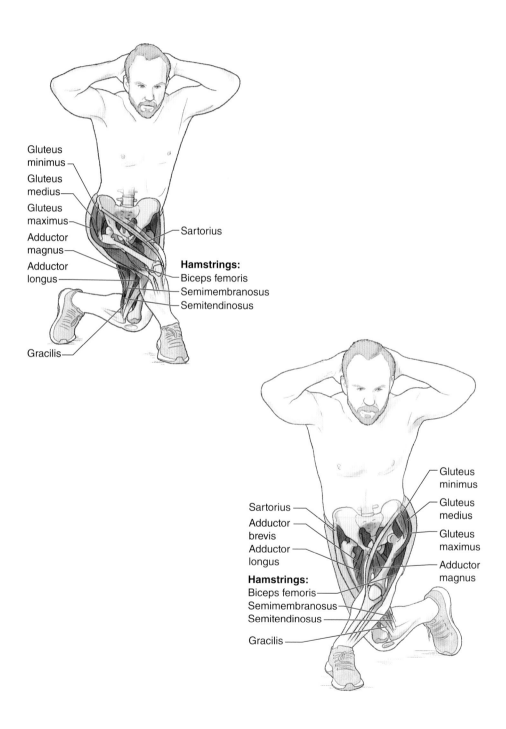

Gluteus minimus
Gluteus medius
Gluteus maximus
Adductor magnus
Adductor longus
Sartorius
Hamstrings:
Biceps femoris
Semimembranosus
Semitendinosus
Gracilis

Sartorius
Adductor brevis
Adductor longus
Hamstrings:
Biceps femoris
Semimembranosus
Semitendinosus
Gracilis
Gluteus minimus
Gluteus medius
Gluteus maximus
Adductor magnus

Execution

1. Stand tall and place the hands behind the head.
2. Step out to the side with one foot.
3. With the other foot, cross over the wide foot and squat.
4. Push to stand back up and take another step out to the side in the same direction as the first stride.
5. This time, with the same foot that crossed over, cross behind the wide foot and squat.
6. When crossing over or crossing behind, be sure to cross far beyond the knee of the leg that is lunging.
7. Push up and repeat this pattern for the allotted number of repetitions or distance.
8. Perform all repetitions or distance toward one side and then switch directions.

Muscles Involved

Primary: Gluteus maximus, gluteus medius, gluteus minimus, adductor magnus, adductor brevis, adductor longus, hamstrings (semitendinosus, semimembranosus, biceps femoris)

Secondary: Gracilis, sartorius

HOCKEY FOCUS

Similar to crossing over on the ice, this drill uses a low lunging position to move laterally. It also stretches the muscles used in this movement pattern.

IT BAND WALK

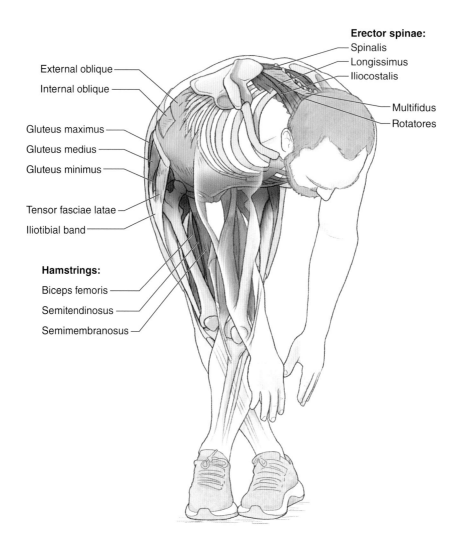

External oblique

Internal oblique

Gluteus maximus

Gluteus medius

Gluteus minimus

Tensor fasciae latae

Iliotibial band

Hamstrings:

Biceps femoris

Semitendinosus

Semimembranosus

Erector spinae:

Spinalis

Longissimus

Iliocostalis

Multifidus

Rotatores

Execution

1. Stand with feet shoulder-width apart and arms down at the sides.
2. Step one foot out to the side.
3. With the other foot, cross over the wide foot.
4. Place the feet side by side.
5. Turn the shoulders and reach down to the outside of the leg that crossed over.
6. Continue in this manner for the allotted number of repetitions or distance.
7. Switch directions and cross with the other foot.

Muscles Involved

Primary: Iliotibial band, hamstrings (semitendinosus, semimembranosus, biceps femoris), gluteus maximus, gluteus medius, gluteus minimus, erector spinae (iliocostalis, longissimus, spinalis)

Secondary: Tensor fasciae latae, external oblique, internal oblique, rotatores, multifidus, quadratus lumborum

HOCKEY FOCUS

This rotational movement stretches the iliotibial band, which often gets tight from skating and externally rotating. Keeping this band stretched can prevent knee and hip discomfort.

BALANCE

Balance is critical to all hockey activities. Players must balance from the time they first touch the ice until they leave it. Skating, shooting, checking, and every other activity on the ice involves balance. Despite the fact that balance is fundamental in sports and especially in hockey, it is often overlooked and not a focus of training. Improving your balance can improve every aspect of your game.

The muscles critical to achieving balance are the accessory muscles of the pelvis and lower extremities. These include the small adductors of the hip (pectineus, adductor longus, adductor brevis, and gracilis), sartorius, short external rotators of the hip (gemelli and piriformis), tensor fasciae latae, peroneal muscles, anterior and posterior tibialis muscles, flexor hallucis longus and lesser toe flexors, and intrinsic muscles of the foot. While the major muscle groups (gluteals, quadriceps, hamstrings, and gastrocnemius) are involved, they are not as critical.

Perform the exercises in this chapter barefoot or in a flexible and nonsupportive shoe. This makes the body work to achieve balance and eliminates reliance on supportive foot wear.

STAR EXCURSION

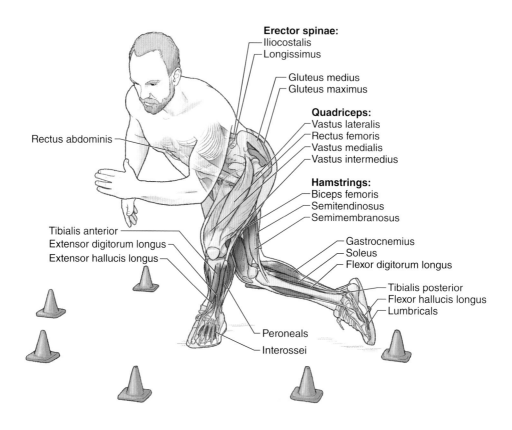

Erector spinae:
Iliocostalis
Longissimus

Gluteus medius
Gluteus maximus

Quadriceps:
Vastus lateralis
Rectus femoris
Vastus medialis
Vastus intermedius

Hamstrings:
Biceps femoris
Semitendinosus
Semimembranosus

Gastrocnemius
Soleus
Flexor digitorum longus

Tibialis posterior
Flexor hallucis longus
Lumbricals

Rectus abdominis

Tibialis anterior
Extensor digitorum longus
Extensor hallucis longus

Peroneals
Interossei

Left limb stance

Anterior

Anterolateral   Anteromedial

Lateral   Medial

Posterolateral   Posteromedial

Posterior

Right limb stance

Anterior

Anteromedial   Anterolateral

Lateral   Medial

Posteromedial   Posterolateral

Posterior

Execution

1. Set up eight cones in a star shape.
2. Stand on one foot in the center of the star. Raise the other foot off the ground, keeping the leg straight and toe pointed.
3. With the lifted foot, reach out and touch the cone at each location: anterolateral, anterior, anteromedial, lateral, medial, posterolateral, posterior, and posteromedial. One complete path around the star equals one repetition.
4. Perform the allotted number of repetitions and then switch legs.

Muscles Involved

Primary: Gastrocnemius, soleus, tibialis anterior, extensor hallucis longus, extensor digitorum longus, flexor hallucis longus, flexor digitorum longus, tibialis posterior, peroneals, interossei, lumbricals

Secondary: Gluteus maximus, gluteus medius, hamstrings (semitendinosus, semimembranosus, biceps femoris), quadriceps (rectus femoris, vastus lateralis, vastus medialis, vastus intermedius), erector spinae (iliocostalis, longissimus, spinalis), rectus abdominis

HOCKEY FOCUS

The ability to skate and play hockey requires being stable on one foot and leg. Your ability reach out with the foot in all directions while maintaining balance indicates how effective on a single-leg you will be on the ice. Lapses in balance can lead to decreased performance or to injury.

BALANCE BOARD ISOMETRIC SQUAT

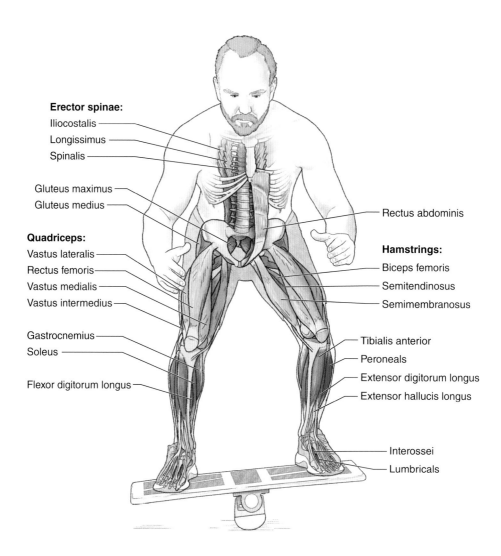

Erector spinae:
Iliocostalis
Longissimus
Spinalis

Gluteus maximus
Gluteus medius

Quadriceps:
Vastus lateralis
Rectus femoris
Vastus medialis
Vastus intermedius

Gastrocnemius
Soleus

Flexor digitorum longus

Rectus abdominis

Hamstrings:
Biceps femoris
Semitendinosus
Semimembranosus

Tibialis anterior
Peroneals
Extensor digitorum longus
Extensor hallucis longus

Interossei
Lumbricals

Execution

1. Stand with feet shoulder-width apart on a balance board. Choose a size that is challenging; the more rounded the bottom of the balance board, the more difficult the exercise will be.
2. Maintain a quarter squat on the board while keeping the sides of the board from touching the ground.
3. Perform for the allotted time.

Muscles Involved

Primary: Gastrocnemius, soleus, tibialis anterior, extensor hallucis longus, extensor digitorum longus, flexor hallucis longus, flexor digitorum longus, tibialis posterior, peroneals, plantar interossei, dorsal interossei, lumbricals

Secondary: Gluteus maximus, gluteus medius, hamstrings (semitendinosus, semimembranosus, biceps femoris), quadriceps (rectus femoris, vastus lateralis, vastus medialis, vastus intermedius), erector spinae (iliocostalis, longissimus, spinalis), rectus abdominis

HOCKEY FOCUS

The ability to hold a low position on the ice is critical. To be able to do so while absorbing forces that attempt to pull the body off center is even more critical. Rarely is a player engaged on the ice without facing some external force that can disturb his or her center of gravity. The better the player is at balancing in this low position, the better it will translate into more effective play.

SINGLE-LEG LATERAL ARM REACH

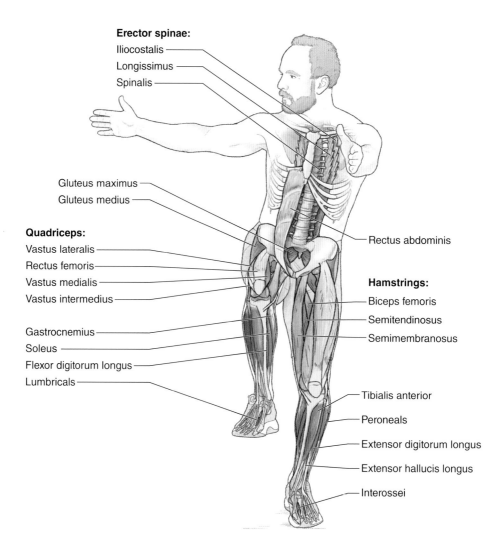

Erector spinae:
Iliocostalis
Longissimus
Spinalis

Gluteus maximus
Gluteus medius

Quadriceps:
Vastus lateralis
Rectus femoris
Vastus medialis
Vastus intermedius

Gastrocnemius
Soleus
Flexor digitorum longus
Lumbricals

Rectus abdominis

Hamstrings:
Biceps femoris
Semitendinosus
Semimembranosus

Tibialis anterior

Peroneals

Extensor digitorum longus

Extensor hallucis longus

Interossei

Execution

1. Stand on one foot. Lift the other leg so the knee is at hip height.
2. Raise the arms to shoulder height with palms together but do not interlock the fingers.
3. While standing on one leg, reach out to the side as far as possible with one arm, slowly rotating the shoulders in that direction and watching the hand move the entire time.
4. Keep the stationary arm straight ahead.
5. Return the moving arm to the center and repeat with the other arm.
6. Repeat for the allotted number of repetitions per side.
7. Switch legs and repeat.

Muscles Involved

Primary: Gastrocnemius, soleus, tibialis anterior, extensor hallucis longus, extensor digitorum longus, flexor hallucis longus, flexor digitorum longus, tibialis posterior, peroneals, plantar interossei, dorsal interossei, lumbricals

Secondary: Gluteus maximus, gluteus medius, hamstrings (semitendinosus, semimembranosus, biceps femoris), quadriceps (rectus femoris, vastus lateralis, vastus medialis, vastus intermedius), erector spinae (iliocostalis, longissimus, spinalis), rectus abdominis

HOCKEY FOCUS

Because players and the puck are constantly in motion, it is important to remain stable on one leg while visually tracking. Although this drill develops visual tracking skills in a controlled setting off the ice, players can easily transfer the skill to movement on the ice.

VARIATIONS

Balance Challenges

- Close one eye.
- Close both eyes.
- Quickly move the arm to the side and back.

ISOMETRIC SPLIT SQUAT WITH EXTERNAL PERTURBATION

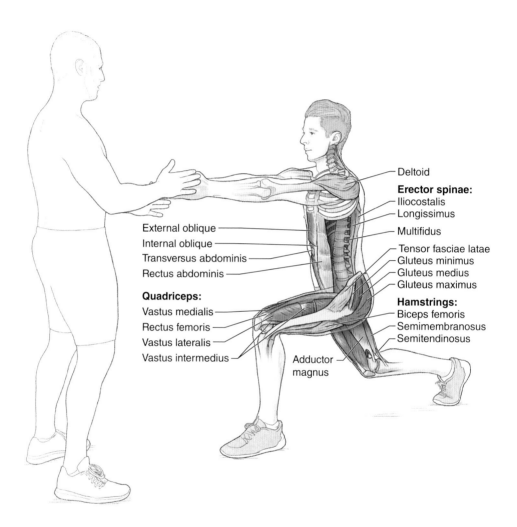

Deltoid

Erector spinae:
Iliocostalis
Longissimus

Multifidus

Tensor fasciae latae
Gluteus minimus
Gluteus medius
Gluteus maximus

Hamstrings:
Biceps femoris
Semimembranosus
Semitendinosus

External oblique
Internal oblique
Transversus abdominis
Rectus abdominis

Quadriceps:
Vastus medialis
Rectus femoris
Vastus lateralis
Vastus intermedius

Adductor magnus

Execution

1. Assume a long lunge position with the front leg bent at 90 degrees and the back leg at about 120 degrees.

2. Hold the arms straight out in front at shoulder height with the hands clasped.

3. A partner stands in front of you and puts pressure in all directions on the outsides, tops, and bottoms of your hands.

4. Be sure to keep the arms straight while your partner applies pressure.

5. Hold for the allotted time. Switch the leg positions.

Muscles Involved

Primary: Quadriceps (rectus femoris, vastus lateralis, vastus medialis, vastus intermedius), gluteus maximus, gluteus medius, multifidus, transversus abdominis, internal oblique, external oblique

Secondary: Hamstrings (semitendinosus, semimembranosus, biceps femoris), gluteus minimus, adductor magnus, deltoid, rectus abdominis, erector spinae (iliocostalis, longissimus, spinalis), tensor fasciae latae

HOCKEY FOCUS

A player needs to be able to skate and absorb contact and still maintain pace, speed, and agility. During a game, external forces will act on the upper body, especially during battles along the boards. This drill develops the critical ability to balance and move while maintaining puck possession or checking someone.

VARIATION

Isometric Split Squat With External Perturbation and Eyes Closed

In the lunge position, close one eye and perform the exercise. For more challenge, close both eyes.

ISOMETRIC SQUAT WITH STICK AND EXTERNAL PERTURBATION

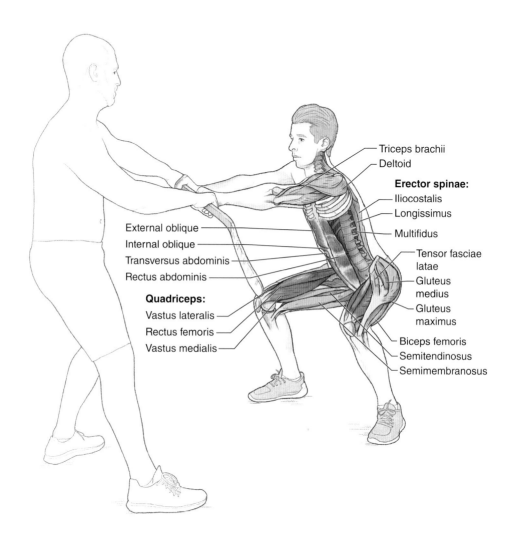

Triceps brachii
Deltoid

Erector spinae:
Iliocostalis
Longissimus

Multifidus

External oblique
Internal oblique
Transversus abdominis
Rectus abdominis

Quadriceps:
Vastus lateralis
Rectus femoris
Vastus medialis

Tensor fasciae latae
Gluteus medius
Gluteus maximus

Biceps femoris
Semitendinosus
Semimembranosus

Execution

1. Assume a squat stance with feet shoulder-width apart, hamstrings parallel to the ground, chest upright, and the back flat.
2. Hold a stick in both hands at arm's length and shoulder height using the most comfortable grip.
3. Your partner grabs the stick and applies pressure and movement in all directions on the stick.
4. Maintain the squat position and fight to keep the stick in the neutral starting position without losing your balance.
5. Hold for the allotted time.

Muscles Involved

Primary: Rectus abdominis, transversus abdominis, internal oblique, external oblique, rectus femoris, vastus medialis, vastus lateralis

Secondary: Gluteus medius, gluteus maximus, biceps femoris, semitendinosus, semimembranosus, erector spinae (iliocostalis, longissimus, spinalis), deltoid, triceps brachii,

HOCKEY FOCUS

Hockey involves a constant battle for position that requires reading and reacting and transferring energy from the upper body to the lower body and vice versa. This drill develops strength and the ability to transfer energy while in an athletic position, which are vital for stability while shooting, passing, or skating when being hit from various angles.

This skill is also important when forces work to keep you from where you want to go. Goalies use this skill when they need to be solid on their skates while moving through the crease, able to absorb the external force of pucks hitting, and when they reach to save.

VARIATION

Isometric Squat With Stick and External Perturbation and Eyes Closed

In the squat, close one eye and perform the drill. For more challenge, close both eyes.

SINGLE-LEG OVERHEAD MEDICINE BALL LATERAL SLAM

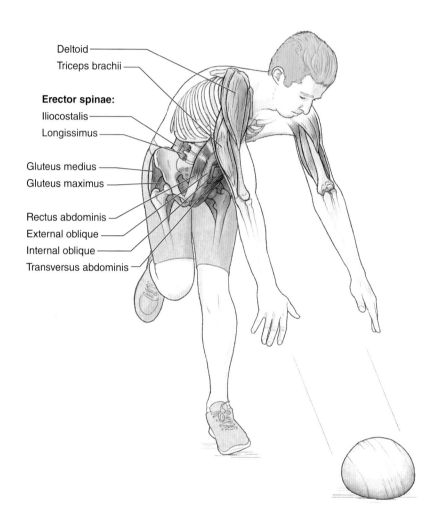

Deltoid

Triceps brachii

Erector spinae:

Iliocostalis

Longissimus

Gluteus medius

Gluteus maximus

Rectus abdominis

External oblique

Internal oblique

Transversus abdominis

Execution

1. Stand on one leg with the hip and knee of the free extremity bent to 90 degrees. Hold a no-bounce medicine ball overhead in both hands.
2. Rotate the torso and throw the medicine ball down to the outside of one leg.
3. Squat on the single leg and pick up the medicine ball. Bring it overhead.
4. Throw it down to the opposite side.
5. Repeat for the allotted number of repetitions for each side. Switch legs.

Muscles Involved

Primary: Rectus abdominis, transversus abdominis, internal oblique, external oblique

Secondary: Gluteus medius, gluteus maximus, erector spinae (iliocostalis, longissimus, spinalis), deltoids, triceps brachii

HOCKEY FOCUS

The ability to generate torque and rotational power while on a single leg is critical while shooting. Being able to plant on a single leg and transfer power from the planted leg through the body and into the arms is what creates the speed of the shot. Balancing on a single blade is paramount while generating the force in the body and then transmitting it through the stick and into the puck.

SINGLE-LEG STICKHANDLING ON BOSU

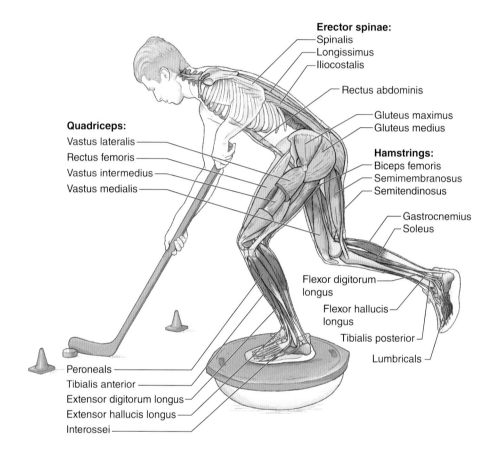

Erector spinae:
Spinalis
Longissimus
Iliocostalis

Rectus abdominis

Gluteus maximus
Gluteus medius

Hamstrings:
Biceps femoris
Semimembranosus
Semitendinosus

Gastrocnemius
Soleus

Quadriceps:
Vastus lateralis
Rectus femoris
Vastus intermedius
Vastus medialis

Flexor digitorum longus

Flexor hallucis longus

Tibialis posterior

Lumbricals

Peroneals
Tibialis anterior
Extensor digitorum longus
Extensor hallucis longus
Interossei

Execution

1. Balance in a single-leg quarter squat on the flat side of a stability trainer, such as a BOSU ball. Use the free leg to maintain balance.
2. At the same time stickhandle a ball or puck around cones laid out in the front of you and to the side.
3. Move the ball or puck in a specific pattern or randomly through the cones.
4. Perform for the allotted time. Switch legs.

Muscles Involved

Primary: Gastrocnemius, soleus, tibialis anterior, extensor hallucis longus, extensor digitorum longus, flexor hallucis longus, flexor digitorum longus, tibialis posterior, peroneals, plantar interossei, dorsal interossei, lumbricals

Secondary: Gluteus maximus, gluteus medius, hamstrings (semitendinosus, semimembranosus, biceps femoris), quadriceps (rectus femoris, vastus lateralis, vastus medialis, vastus intermedius), erector spinae (iliocostalis, longissimus, spinalis), rectus abdominis

HOCKEY FOCUS

All players need to be able to stickhandle during any on-ice situation while maintaining balance and focus and encountering external instabilities. Hockey is played on two legs sometimes, such as when moving to make a play with the puck, but skating, stickhandling, and absorbing and controlling contact while on a single leg often comes into play.

VARIATIONS

Single-Leg Stickhandling on BOSU with Eye Closed

Perform the single-leg stickhandling exercise on a stability trainer with one eye closed.

FOUR-POINT KNEELING ON BALL

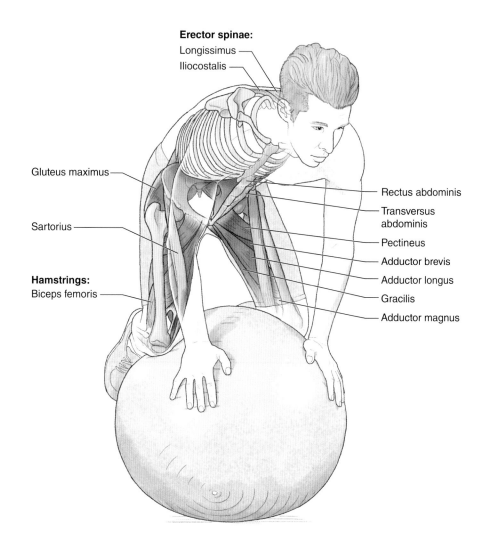

Erector spinae:
Longissimus
Iliocostalis

Gluteus maximus

Sartorius

Hamstrings:
Biceps femoris

Rectus abdominis

Transversus abdominis

Pectineus

Adductor brevis

Adductor longus

Gracilis

Adductor magnus

Execution

1. Place both hands on an exercise ball that ranges from 55 to 75 centimeters.
2. Lift one knee toward the ball and place it on the ball slightly behind the hands.
3. Once you feel comfortable in this position, lift the other knee up to the ball. Knees are about shoulder-width apart.
4. Balance on the ball in this four-point stance for the allotted time.
5. If you fall off, stop the time and continue from the point when the time was stopped.
6. The larger the ball, the easier the drill.

Muscles Involved

Primary: Adductor magnus, adductor longus, adductor brevis, pectineus, gracilis

Secondary: Gluteus maximus, hamstrings (semitendinosus, semimembranosus, biceps femoris), sartorius, erector spinae (iliocostalis, longissimus, spinalis), transversus abdominis, rectus abdominis

HOCKEY FOCUS

Coordination and balance during quick acceleration or when engaging in contact can be challenging. The core, lower body, and upper body need to work together in unstable environments to create a strong presence on the ice while skating. In conjunction with the demands of skating itself, a player may need to simultaneously evade players or checks; maintain momentum while being checked or fighting for a puck; or even maintain momentum while delivering a check.

VARIATIONS

Three-Point Kneeling on Ball

After balancing on four points on the ball, take one hand off the ball. Hold for the allotted time. Switch hands.

Two-Point Kneeling on Ball

After balancing on four points on the ball, take both hands off the ball. Lift the chest so it is perpendicular to the ground.

Two-Point Kneeling on Ball With Catch and Throw

Once you are adept at balancing in the two-point kneeling position, have a partner throw a tennis ball to you from various angles. Catch the ball, switching hands with each catch. Once you can catch the tennis ball, have your partner throw a weighted medicine ball to you.

8

CORE STABILITY

The core muscles are used in nearly every facet of playing hockey. The abdominals—the internal and external obliques, transversus abdominis, and rectus abdominis (figure 8.1)—are the muscles most people think about when they consider the core. However, the core also includes key muscles in the back, such as the erector spinae, quadratus lumborum, and multifidus, as well as the hip and the gluteal muscles, such as the gluteus minimus, gluteus medius, and iliopsoas. The core muscles stabilize the upper body during skating, battling, and checking. They also provide the power needed when shooting and assist in providing power and speed during skating. Crossing over and changing direction when skating requires the core muscles and activates them. Goalies need to have a powerful and well-conditioned core because they use the core muscles constantly. Goalies use their posterior core while maintaining a ready position, their lateral core muscles when shifting side to side and when elevating their arms, and their anterior core when getting into a butterfly position or performing a kick save.

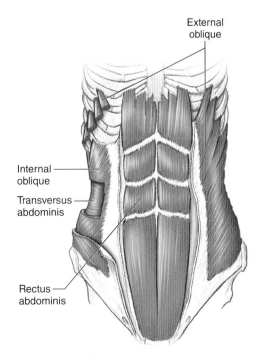

External oblique

Internal oblique

Transversus abdominis

Rectus abdominis

FIGURE 8.1 Abdominal muscles.

SIDE BRIDGE WITH ABDUCTION

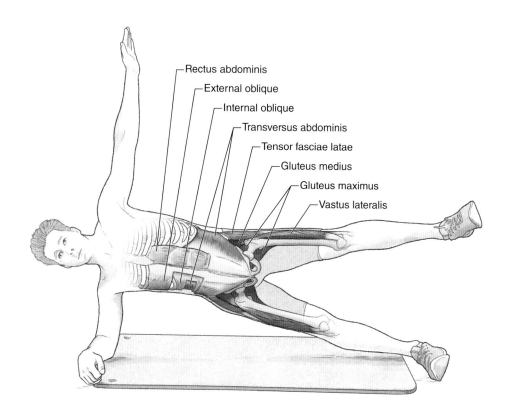

Rectus abdominis

External oblique

Internal oblique

Transversus abdominis

Tensor fasciae latae

Gluteus medius

Gluteus maximus

Vastus lateralis

Execution

1. Place a forearm flat on the floor so that it is perpendicular to the body and the elbow is directly under the shoulder. Stack the feet on top of each another. Press into the floor with the forearm and the side of the bottom foot.
2. Raise the hips until they are aligned with the rest of the body. The body should be in a straight line from the head to the heels. The top shoulder should not roll forward.
3. Lift the top foot, keeping the leg straight.
4. Hold for the allotted time or perform the specified number of repetitions of leg raises. Switch sides.

Muscles Involved

Primary: Transversus abdominis, gluteus medius, gluteus maximus, vastus lateralis, tensor fasciae latae

Secondary: Rectus abdominis, external oblique, internal oblique

HOCKEY FOCUS

Players can perform side bridges with a straight arm to emphasize the lateral aspect of the core and shoulder stability. Shoulder stability is necessary for absorbing and delivering contact and for fending off an opponent. By performing the abduction raise, we are working contralaterally and connecting the entire core.

VARIATION

Side Bridge Reach Through

Perform the side bridge, keeping the feet together. With the top arm, reach through and under the body, rotating at the hips. Bring the arm back to point to the ceiling. You can hold a weight in the hand that is reaching through.

FRONT BRIDGE WITH BAND OPEN-UP

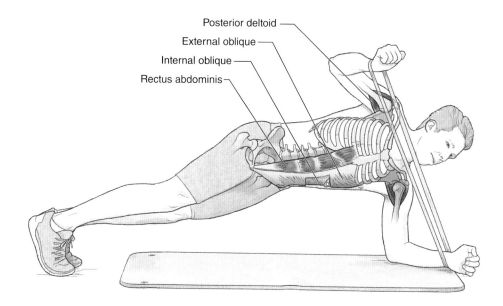

Posterior deltoid

External oblique

Internal oblique

Rectus abdominis

Execution

1. Place a miniband around both wrists. Position the forearms on the ground so the elbows are directly under the shoulders and the feet are together.
2. Press into the ground with the forearms and toes to elevate the body, keeping it in a straight line from head to heels.
3. From this position, lift one arm up and to the side. The arm is at a 90-degree angle at the elbow and shoulder. Rotate the trunk.
4. Bring the arm back under the body to the start position and then rotate and lift the other arm.

Muscles Involved

Primary: Rectus abdominis, posterior deltoid

Secondary: Internal oblique, external oblique

HOCKEY FOCUS

This drill develops shoulder stability and strength. A player driving the net or positioning and fighting off an opposing player requires this movement to push off and gain space.

VARIATION

Front-Bridge Hip Raise

From the front-bridge position, lift the hips up and back, extending at the shoulders. Return to the start position.

DEAD BUG WITH ISOMETRIC PUSH

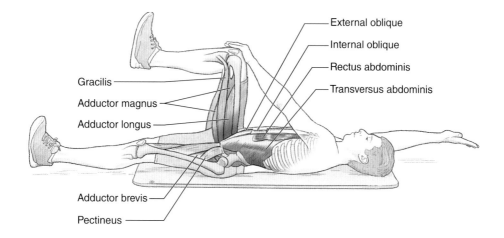

External oblique

Internal oblique

Rectus abdominis

Transversus abdominis

Gracilis

Adductor magnus

Adductor longus

Adductor brevis

Pectineus

Execution

1. Lie on the back with the knees and hips bent to 90-degree angles.

2. Extend one leg straight out in front and extend the opposite arm overhead.

3. At the same time, use the other hand to press against the bent knee. Push the hand against the knee and also push back against the hand. Hold for a two count and release.

4. Draw in the abdominals and keep the low back flat against the ground.

5. Switch sides and continue. Perform the allotted number of repetitions per side.

Muscles Involved

Primary: Rectus abdominis, transversus abdominis

Secondary: External oblique, internal oblique, adductor magnus, adductor longus, adductor brevis, pectineus, gracilis

HOCKEY FOCUS

Many hockey players have too much inward curve in their lower spine, known as excessive lumbar lordosis, which is caused by too much anterior pelvic tilt. This exercise works the deep and lower muscles of the core, enabling the athlete to relieve the stress on the lower back and neutralize the anterior pelvic tilt.

VARIATION

Dead Bug With Elastic Band

Secure an elastic band around the tops and bottoms of the feet. Perform the dead bug movement against the resistance of the band.

SUPERMAN MEDICINE BALL TOSS

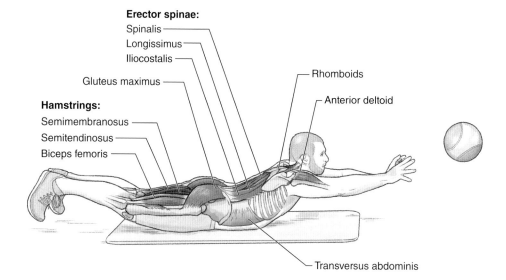

Erector spinae:
Spinalis
Longissimus
Iliocostalis

Gluteus maximus

Rhomboids

Anterior deltoid

Hamstrings:
Semimembranosus
Semitendinosus
Biceps femoris

Transversus abdominis

Execution

1. Lie facedown with the legs straight. Hold a medicine ball under the chin with your hands.
2. Lift the chest and legs. Throw the ball from under the chin.
3. Try to elevate the chest to throw the ball up and out as far as possible.
4. Have a partner roll the ball back.

Muscles Involved

Primary: Anterior deltoid, erector spinae (iliocostalis, longissimus, spinalis), gluteus maximus, hamstrings (semitendinosus, semimembranosus, biceps femoris)

Secondary: Transversus abdominis, rhomboids

HOCKEY FOCUS

Although not an overhead sport, hockey does require upper-body power for arm swing propulsion, shooting, and checking. This drill helps to develop this power and increases strength through the contraction of the lower back at the same time as the throw.

VARIATIONS

Overhead Superman Medicine Ball Toss

Perform the same movement except throw the medicine ball from overhead like a soccer throw-in.

Superman

Lie facedown with the legs straight, toes flexed toward the head (dorsiflexed), and arms extended overhead. Lift the arms and legs at the same time, keeping the head down.

HIP BRIDGE SQUEEZE

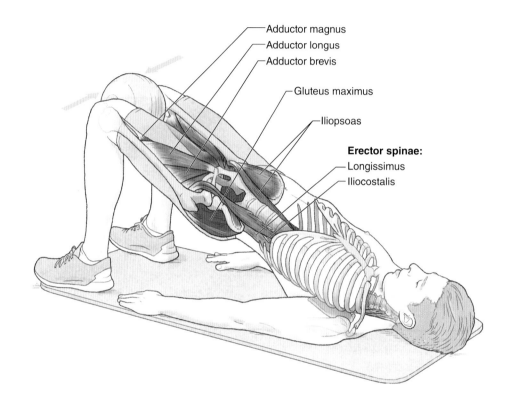

Adductor magnus

Adductor longus

Adductor brevis

Gluteus maximus

Iliopsoas

Erector spinae:

Longissimus

Iliocostalis

Execution

1. Lie on your back with the feet flat on the ground under the knees. Place a soft 6- to 10-inch (15-25 cm) diameter ball between the knees.
2. Lift the hips to form a straight line from chin to knees.
3. Squeeze the ball between the knees. Pause for a two count and release, keeping the ball between the knees.
4. Lower the hips to the floor.
5. Repeat the bridge and squeeze for the allotted number of repetitions.

Muscles Involved

Primary: Gluteus maximus, adductor longus, adductor magnus, adductor brevis, iliopsoas

Secondary: Erector spinae (iliocostalis, longissimus, spinalis)

HOCKEY FOCUS

Because of the demands skating and shooting place on the back, the hips often become misaligned, which can cause compensatory movement patterns that could lead to injury and inefficiency. This drill addresses the alignment of the hips and works to strengthen and stabilize them.

VARIATION

Hip Bridge Squeeze With Hold

Perform the squeeze for an allotted amount of time while maintaining the hips-up position.

BIRD DOG

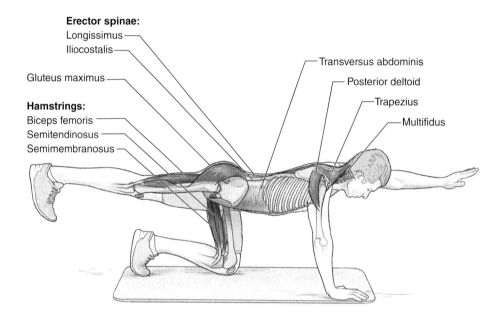

Erector spinae:
Longissimus
Iliocostalis

Gluteus maximus

Hamstrings:
Biceps femoris
Semitendinosus
Semimembranosus

Transversus abdominis

Posterior deltoid

Trapezius

Multifidus

Execution

1. Kneel on all fours on the ground, knees directly under the hips and hands directly under the shoulders. Hold the head in a neutral position so the spine is straight from the top of the head to the sacrum.

2. Extend one leg back with the toes flexed toward the head (dorsiflexed). Extend the arm on the opposite side straight ahead so the body is in line from head to heel.

3. Hold this top position for the allotted time, and then return the knee and hand to the starting position.

4. Repeat on the opposite side for the allotted time.

Muscles Involved

Primary: Gluteus maximus, hamstrings (semitendinosus, semimembranosus, biceps femoris), multifidus, posterior deltoid, trapezius

Secondary: Transversus abdominis, erector spinae (iliocostalis, longissimus, spinalis)

HOCKEY FOCUS

This exercise strengthens the entire posterior chain. Developing the posterior chain helps players in extension so they can drive harder and extend the leg farther when propelling themselves while skating. In addition, this helps in blocking out opposing players along the boards and battling in front of the net.

GIANT CIRCLE WITH CABLE OR BAND

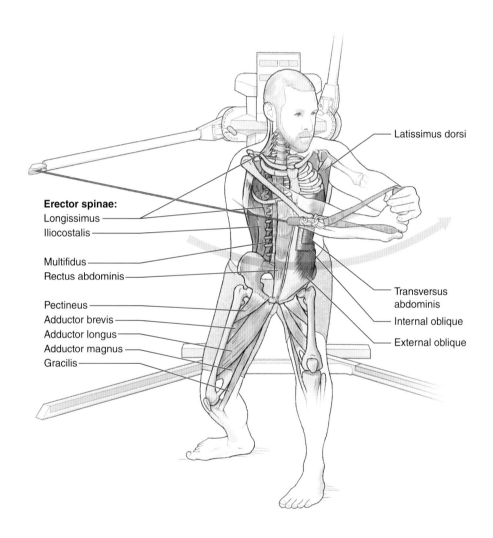

Latissimus dorsi

Erector spinae:
Longissimus
Iliocostalis

Multifidus
Rectus abdominis

Pectineus
Adductor brevis
Adductor longus
Adductor magnus
Gracilis

Transversus abdominis

Internal oblique

External oblique

Execution

1. Stand tall with the feet shoulder-width apart. Grab a cable or band with the arms extended and the cable or band perpendicular to the body. Pull it with straight arms so that there is no slack.

2. Pull the cable or band overhead in a clockwise arc and continue the circle, maintaining straight arms so it goes low and back to the starting position.

3. Complete the allotted number of repetitions, and then repeat in a counterclockwise motion.

4. As the cable or band moves in a circle around the body, the body should rise and descend with the circle. Flex and extend at the knees, but keep the torso upright.

Muscles Involved

Primary: Internal oblique, external oblique, multifidus, transversus abdominis

Secondary: Rectus abdominis, erector spinae (iliocostalis, longissimus, spinalis), adductor magnus, adductor longus, adductor brevis, pectineus, gracilis, latissimus dorsi

HOCKEY FOCUS

This drill requires stability during movement, a key characteristic of skating. As the arms move the band and the knees flex and extend, keep the midsection solid and upright. Avoid arching the back. Move deliberately and under control.

WINDMILL

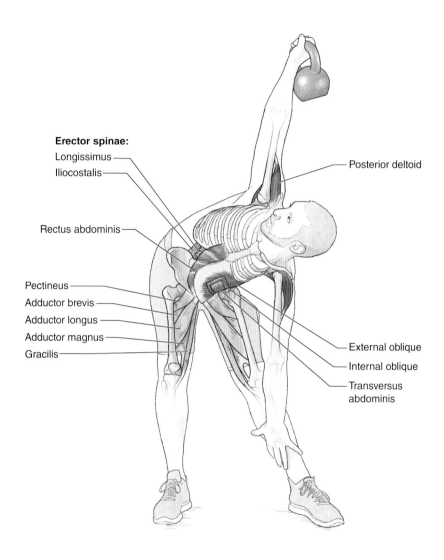

Erector spinae:
Longissimus
Iliocostalis

Posterior deltoid

Rectus abdominis

Pectineus
Adductor brevis
Adductor longus
Adductor magnus
Gracilis

External oblique

Internal oblique

Transversus
abdominis

Execution

1. Stand with the feet shoulder-width apart. Hold a kettlebell in one hand at shoulder height. Press the kettlebell overhead with a straight arm and hold it there for the duration of the exercise.

2. Place the free hand on the inside of the thigh. Turn the toes of the nonkettlebell side out at a 45-degree angle.

3. To move, turn the shoulders toward the kettlebell side. Push the hip out to the kettlebell side and slide the free hand down the leg toward the ankle. The torso will naturally bend laterally as the hand descends.

4. Descend as far as flexibility at the shoulder and back allow, and then return to the upright position.

5. Perform the allotted number of repetitions on one side before switching to the other side.

Muscles Involved

Primary: Rectus abdominis, transversus abdominis, internal oblique, external oblique, posterior deltoid

Secondary: Erector spinae (iliocostalis, longissimus, spinalis), adductor magnus, adductor longus, adductor brevis, pectineus, gracilis

HOCKEY FOCUS

Many hockey movements, such as shooting and pivoting, require a high level of flexibility and torque in the core as well as hip mobility at the same time. This is a high-level drill because it combines many hockey movements and connects the entire body. It is a great tool for assessing a player's movement patterns.

VARIATION

Kneeling Kettlebell Windmill

Kneel on the leg on the kettlebell side, keeping the other leg straight.

HYDRANT

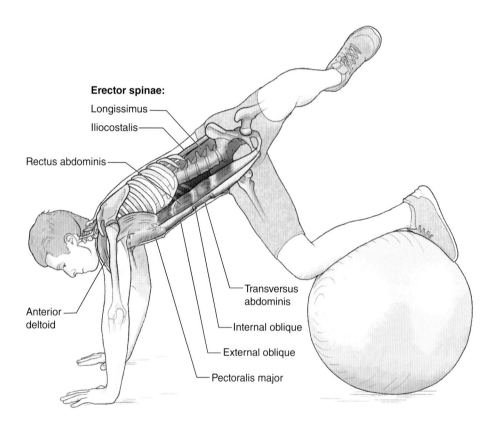

Erector spinae:
Longissimus
Iliocostalis

Rectus abdominis

Anterior
deltoid

Transversus
abdominis

Internal oblique

External oblique

Pectoralis major

Execution

1. Assume a push-up position with the shins on a stability ball and the hands on the ground. Draw the ball in by raising the hips and bending the knees so that they are directly under the hips and the shins remain on the ball.

2. Rotate the hips to one side while taking the top leg off the bottom, opening up to the side.

3. Rotate the hips back to the start so both shins are on the ball.

4. Rotate the hips to the other side.

Muscles Involved

Primary: Rectus abdominis, transversus abdominis, internal oblique, external oblique

Secondary: Multifidus, erector spinae (iliocostalis, longissimus, spinalis), pectoralis major, anterior deltoid

HOCKEY FOCUS

Hip and low-back mobility and rotation are paramount in creating high levels of force and power on a shot. Also, when a player digs in along the boards for a puck, the constant battle for positioning requires strength and leverage. This drill increases mobility, rotation, and strength of the hips and low back and also improves the ability to open the hips while skating and pivoting.

HALF-KNEELING MEDICINE BALL CHOP

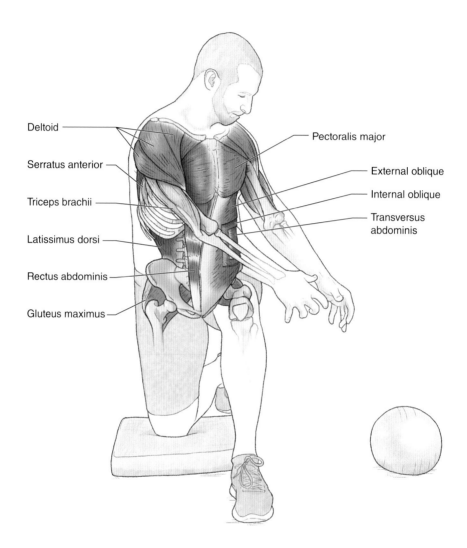

Deltoid

Serratus anterior

Triceps brachii

Latissimus dorsi

Rectus abdominis

Gluteus maximus

Pectoralis major

External oblique

Internal oblique

Transversus abdominis

Execution

1. Lunge forward and kneel on a soft pad with one leg up so it is bent at a 90-degree angle at the knee and the hip and the foot is flat on the ground.

2. Hold a medicine ball in both hands. Bring it high over the shoulder opposite the front knee.

3. Diagonally rotate the torso and arms and throw the ball down to the ground over the front knee.

4. If near a wall, throw the ball to the ground diagonally so it bounces off the ground, to the wall, and back to you. Or have a partner throw the ball back.

5. Repeat for the allotted number of repetitions and switch sides.

Muscles Involved

Primary: Rectus abdominis, internal oblique, external oblique, latissimus dorsi, deltoids, pectoralis major

Secondary: Triceps brachii, serratus anterior, gluteus maximus

HOCKEY FOCUS

Being able to generate diagonal force across the body leads to a stronger shot. Taking the legs out of this movement necessitates stability, strength, and power of the core to deliver a hard throw, which mimics the shooting pattern.

VARIATION

Chop Alternatives

- Kneel on both knees or stand up.
- Perform the chop using a cable or band attached high to a stanchion.

TRANSVERSE STEP AND PULL

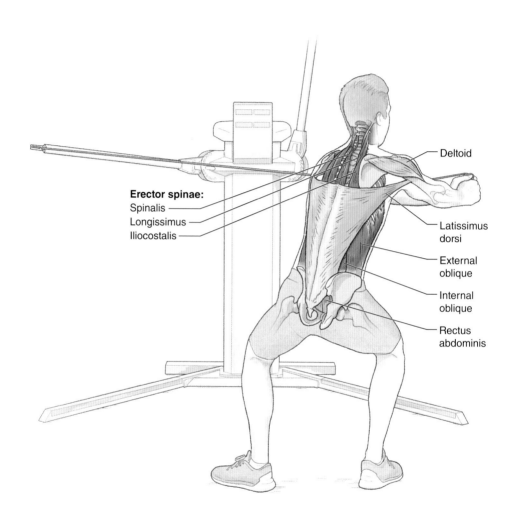

Erector spinae:
Spinalis
Longissimus
Iliocostalis

Deltoid

Latissimus
dorsi

External
oblique

Internal
oblique

Rectus
abdominis

Execution

1. Attach a cable or band to a stanchion. Face the stanchion with the feet shoulder-width apart and grab the cable or band with both hands and pull it so there is no slack.
2. With one foot, step back at a 45-degree angle, opening the hips to that side. At the same time, pull the cable or band with both hands across the body, maintaining straight arms.
3. Step back to the starting position and return the cable or band.
4. Rotate to the other side.
5. Repeat allotted number of repetitions.

Muscles Involved

Primary: External oblique, internal oblique, erector spinae (iliocostalis, longissimus, spinalis)

Secondary: Rectus abdominis, deltoid, latissimus dorsi

HOCKEY FOCUS

Opening up in skating while pivoting at the same time is a common pattern for defensemen covering their gaps and playing their opponents. The transverse step and pull develops that movement pattern while engaging the core and upper body.

VARIATION

Transverse Step and Single-Arm Pull

Grab the cable or band with one hand. Open the hips to the side holding the cable or band by stepping out and back at a 45-degree angle. At the same time, pull the cable or band with the palm facing the center so the back of the fist drives the pull back. Pull all the way with a straight arm across the body. Step back to the center starting position and perform all repetitions on one side before switching to the other side.

LATERAL KICK FROM PUSH-UP POSITION ON STABILITY BALL

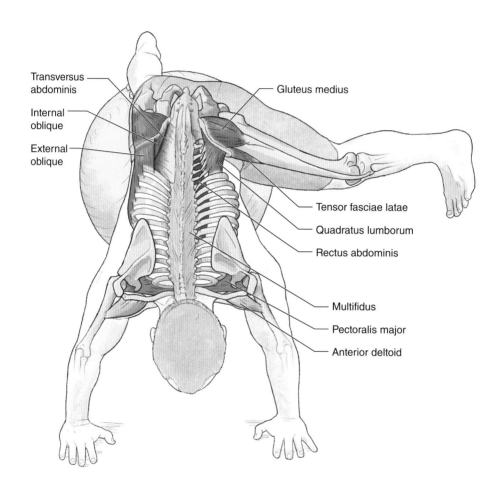

Transversus abdominis

Internal oblique

External oblique

Gluteus medius

Tensor fasciae latae

Quadratus lumborum

Rectus abdominis

Multifidus

Pectoralis major

Anterior deltoid

Execution

1. Place toes on a stability ball and hands on the ground in a decline push-up position.
2. Lift one foot off the ball. With a straight leg, bring the toe of that foot toward the arm on the same side.
3. Return the leg back and place the toes on the ball.
4. Repeat on the other side. Complete the allotted number of repetitions per side.

Muscles Involved

Primary: Rectus abdominis, transversus abdominis, internal oblique, external oblique, tensor fasciae latae, quadratus lumborum, gluteus medius

Secondary: Multifidus, pectoralis major, anterior deltoid

HOCKEY FOCUS

This drill requires a great deal of dynamic mobility and localized strength of the hips plus stabilization of the upper body. The ability to perform this movement leads to better strength on the skates and a stronger grip on the stick. This is important when considering how many awkward positions a player may experience on the ice. It is the ability to stay balanced and stable while being pushed and pulled that promotes better play.

VARIATION

Lateral Kick From Forearm Push-Up Position on Stability Ball

Perform the same movement, except place the forearms instead of the hands on the ground.

INJURY REHABILITATION

9

Injuries are common in collision sports such as hockey. When the playing surface and boundary conditions are as unforgiving as ice and hockey boards and the players and puck are travelling at such a high velocity, it is surprising that more injuries do not occur. Determination, focus, and hard work help athletes become successful at hockey, but those qualities need to be tempered with patience after injuries occur. Athletes need to be smart about rehabilitation and work within their limitations to return to play successfully and prevent future injury.

The most common acute injuries in hockey are foot and hand fractures, lacerations, medial collateral ligament tears, anterior cruciate ligament tears, meniscal tears, acromioclavicular separations, and shoulder dislocations. The most common chronic injuries in hockey include superior labral tears, rotator cuff tearing or irritation, scapholunate ligament tearing in the wrist, triangular fibrocartilage tearing in the wrist, hip labral tearing, athletic pubalgia (sports hernia), and chronic meniscal tearing. Whether their injury is acute or chronic, hockey players should be under the care of qualified medical personnel, therapists, and athletic training staff throughout their recovery.

CONTROLLED ARTICULAR ROTATIONS (CARS) OF THE SHOULDER

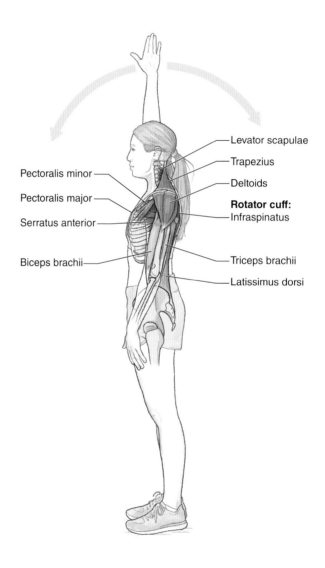

Pectoralis minor

Pectoralis major

Serratus anterior

Biceps brachii

Levator scapulae

Trapezius

Deltoids

Rotator cuff:
Infraspinatus

Triceps brachii

Latissimus dorsi

Execution

1. Stand next to a wall with your arms hanging at your sides. Tense the entire body to isolate the shoulder next to the wall. The arm next to the wall is the working arm.

2. With the thumb of the working arm pointed up, protract the shoulder by reaching forward and up, keeping the arm straight.

3. When you are unable to reach backward, rotate the shoulder and hand so that the palm turns toward the ground.

4. Continue to reach back and retract the shoulder as far as possible.

5. Continue the circle rotation of the shoulder until the hand reaches the hip with the thumb up.

6. Reverse the motion to return to the starting position.

7. Repeat for the allotted number of repetitions for one arm and then switch sides.

Muscles Involved

Primary: Deltoids, serratus anterior, pectoralis minor, trapezius, rhomboids, levator scapulae, rotator cuff (teres minor, infraspinatus, supraspinatus, subscapularis)

Secondary: Latissimus dorsi, biceps brachii, pectoralis major, triceps brachii

HOCKEY FOCUS

This movement stretches and activates the entire shoulder to increase the range of motion, which is necessary for goalies during glove and blocker saves. In addition, it allows for more range of motion on the backend of a player's slapshot and forward motion after the shot comes through.

THORACIC BRIDGE

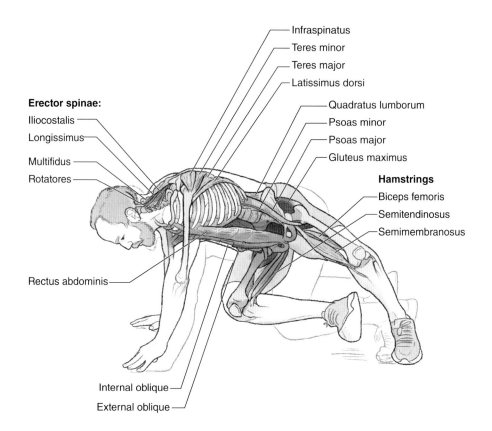

Infraspinatus
Teres minor
Teres major
Latissimus dorsi
Quadratus lumborum
Psoas minor
Psoas major
Gluteus maximus

Erector spinae:
Iliocostalis
Longissimus
Multifidus
Rotatores

Hamstrings
Biceps femoris
Semitendinosus
Semimembranosus

Rectus abdominis

Internal oblique
External oblique

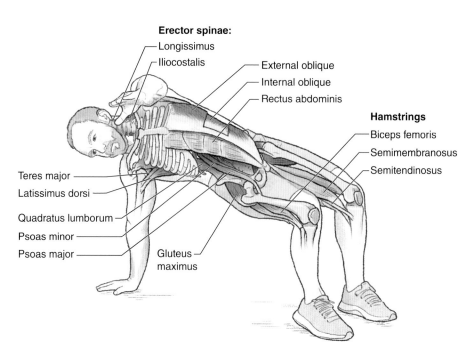

Erector spinae:
Longissimus
Iliocostalis

External oblique
Internal oblique
Rectus abdominis

Hamstrings
Biceps femoris
Semimembranosus
Semitendinosus

Teres major
Latissimus dorsi

Quadratus lumborum
Psoas minor
Psoas major

Gluteus maximus

Execution

1. Kneel on all fours, hands under the shoulders and knees under the hips. Lift your knees off the ground to balance on your hands and toes.

2. Raise the left hand and right foot off the ground.

3. Begin to rotate by bringing the right knee under the body toward the left side. Keep the left arm reaching straight out to the left side.

4. When the right knee clears the body completely, slam the right foot into the ground, driving both hips up to the ceiling.

5. As the hips drive as high as possible, reach out with the left arm and rotate the upper torso to increase the range of motion. The hips should be up and the arm reaching as forcefully and as far as possible. Hold for two to four counts in the top position.

6. Slowly reverse to return to the starting position. Repeat, opening up to the right side.

Muscles Involved

Primary: Erector spinae (iliocostalis, longissimus, spinalis), external oblique, internal oblique, multifidus, rotatores, gluteus maximus

Secondary: Quadratus lumborum, latissimus dorsi, psoas major, psoas minor, rectus abdominis, hamstrings (semitendinosus, semimembranosus, biceps femoris), infraspinatus, teres minor, teres major

HOCKEY FOCUS

This movement requires stabilization of the shoulder and pelvis and increases the range of motion of the reaching shoulder and thoracic spine muscles. This movement expands the rotational range of motion of the entire torso and engages the gluteals to support the bridge. This will help you with skating, pivoting, and shooting.

EXTERNAL ROTATION WITH BAND

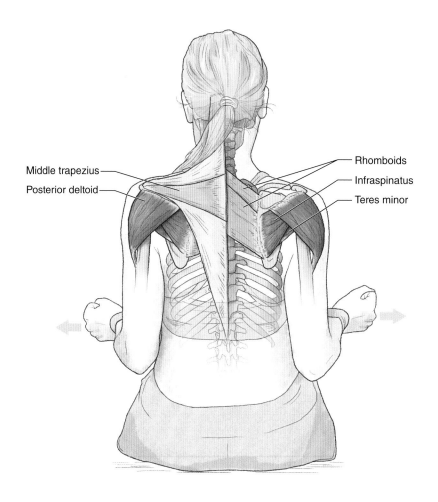

Middle trapezius

Posterior deltoid

Rhomboids

Infraspinatus

Teres minor

Execution

1. Place a miniband around the wrists and grasp the ends in each hand.
2. Sit or stand with your shoulders and back against a wall. If sitting, your legs are straight out in front. Bend your elbows to a 90-degree angle.
3. Keep the upper arms parallel to the ribs.
4. Keep the elbows close to the body and, with a controlled movement, spread the wrists as far as possible.
5. When the band cannot stretch any farther, return to the starting position, again using a controlled movement.
6. Repeat for the allotted number of repetitions.

Muscles Involved

Primary: Posterior deltoid, infraspinatus, teres minor

Secondary: Middle trapezius, rhomboids

HOCKEY FOCUS

This movement develops strength in the back of the shoulder. This stabilizes the shoulder and contributes to being strong on the puck and to stick stability. In addition, a strong posterior shoulder is important for checking and absorbing the forces coming at you from the front, back, and sides. This can help prevent displacement and also provides more force and stability when delivering a check or when counterhitting.

VARIATION

Band Pull Apart

Use a long band that is 1/2 to 1 inch (1.3-2.5 cm) wide. Grasp the band in a shoulder-width grip, keeping tension on the band the whole time. Stretch the band with straight arms. Return the band to the starting position without allowing slack. You also can perform this exercise while holding the band overhead and bringing it down and behind the shoulders.

REBOUND SHOULDER RAISE

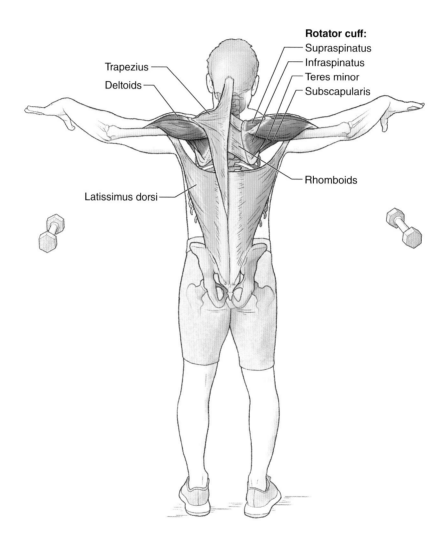

Trapezius

Deltoids

Rotator cuff:
Supraspinatus
Infraspinatus
Teres minor
Subscapularis

Rhomboids

Latissimus dorsi

Execution

1. You can perform the rebound shoulder raise while sitting or standing and with both arms or one arm at a time.

2. Grab a pair of 2- to 5-pound (1-2.3 kg) dumbbells.

3. Raise the arms straight out to the front, sides, or to a 45-degree angle. Or from a bent-over position with the chest down, raise the arms straight out overhead, to the sides, or to the front at a diagonal.

4. From the top position, drop the weight.

5. As soon as the weight is released, reach down to catch it with an overhand grip. Do not let the weight reach the ground.

6. As soon as you catch the weight, bring it back to the starting position. Try to snap the weight up.

7. Pause at the top and then repeat for the allotted number of repetitions.

Muscles Involved

Primary: Deltoids, rotator cuff (teres minor, infraspinatus, supraspinatus, subscapularis)

Secondary: Rhomboids, trapezius, latissimus dorsi

HOCKEY FOCUS

The responsiveness developed by this drill allows you to create and reduce force quickly. It is the ability to instantaneously contract and relax the shoulder that helps stabilize it to absorb impact both in checking and in catching and giving a sharp pass. This is important when pushing off a player and in gaining position or fighting for a puck.

ISOMETRIC IRON CROSS HOLD

Anterior
deltoid

Biceps
brachii

Pectoralis
major

Pectoralis
minor

Execution

1. Stand facing a power rack or doorway.
2. Straighten the arms to the sides at shoulder height.
3. Place forearms on the posts or against the doorframe.
4. Walk the feet away from the rack or doorway and lean the body forward.
5. Hold this straight-line position for the allotted time.

Muscles Involved

Primary: Pectoralis major, pectoralis minor

Secondary: Anterior deltoid, biceps brachii

HOCKEY FOCUS

Hockey often involves facing forward while reaching side to side. This exercise increases range of motion and therefore increases potential for torque on a slapshot and stability when reaching out to the side.

BLACKBURN

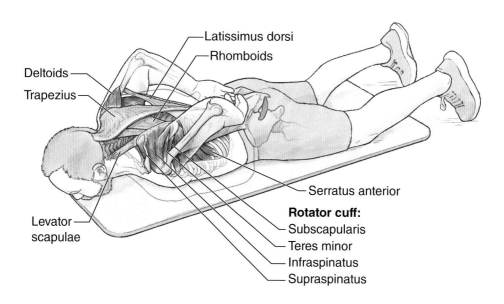

Latissimus dorsi
Rhomboids
Deltoids
Trapezius
Serratus anterior
Rotator cuff:
Subscapularis
Teres minor
Infraspinatus
Supraspinatus
Levator scapulae

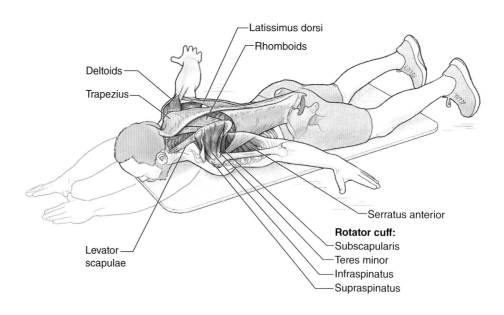

Latissimus dorsi
Rhomboids
Deltoids
Trapezius
Serratus anterior
Rotator cuff:
Subscapularis
Teres minor
Infraspinatus
Supraspinatus
Levator scapulae

Execution

1. Lie facedown on the ground and clasp the hands together behind the lower back.
2. Force the elbows down toward the ground.
3. Raise the elbows as high as possible toward the ceiling.
4. Release the hands from each another.
5. Bring the arms out to the sides and overhead, keeping them off the ground until the hands touch.
6. Lower the arms and reclasp the hands behind the lower back. Repeat for the allotted number of repetitions.

Muscles Involved

Primary: Rotator cuff (teres minor, infraspinatus, supraspinatus, subscapularis), deltoids, serratus anterior

Secondary: Rhomboids, latissimus dorsi, levator scapulae, trapezius

HOCKEY FOCUS

Range of motion and stability are key to avoiding injury when falling to the ice and pushing off an opponent to gain position or protect the puck. This complete movement strengthens and stretches the entire shoulder girdle.

INTERNAL AND EXTERNAL HIP ROTATION WITH BAND

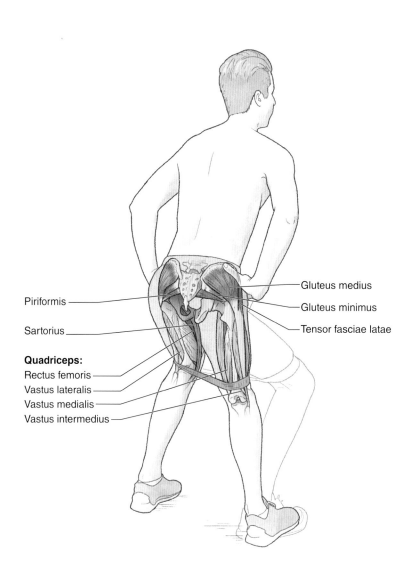

Piriformis

Sartorius

Quadriceps:
Rectus femoris
Vastus lateralis
Vastus medialis
Vastus intermedius

Gluteus medius

Gluteus minimus

Tensor fasciae latae

Execution

1. Stand and wrap a miniband around the tops of the knees.
2. Lower to a quarter-squat position with the feet shoulder-width apart.
3. Keeping the feet as flat as possible, turn one knee in toward the midline of the body.
4. Turn the same knee back to the outside of the body.
5. Repeat for the allotted number of repetitions.
6. Perform one side and then the other and then both at the same time.

Muscles Involved

Primary: Gluteus medius, gluteus minimus, tensor fasciae latae, piriformis

Secondary: Quadriceps (rectus femoris, vastus lateralis, vastus medialis, vastus intermedius), sartorius

HOCKEY FOCUS

The power of the stride comes from a forceful extension of the hip. This exercise focuses on the muscles responsible for explosive power and the muscles that keep the hip stable. Acceleration will be maximized when skating or when a goalie pushes off to cover the angles in the crease.

VARIATIONS

Lateral Walk With Band

Wrap a miniband around the knees, ankles, or both. Stand with straight legs or lower to a quarter squat. Walk laterally to one side, keeping tension on the band. Do not let the feet come together on the recovery. Repeat for the allotted distance or number of repetitions and then walk the other direction.

Band Arc

Wrap a miniband around the knees, ankles, or both. Face forward with feet shoulder-width apart. Bring one foot toward the midline of the body and then reach up and out at a diagonal in the direction of the walk. The foot should make a C shape in the air. Repeat on the other side. Continue for the allotted number of repetitions to each side or for distance. Repeat the drill walking backward.

High–Low Walk

Perform the lateral walk with band, but bring the inside foot (the one closest to the direction of the walk) higher than the back foot. Walk laterally, keeping one foot higher than the other. Repeat in the other direction.

SUPINE LEG WHIP

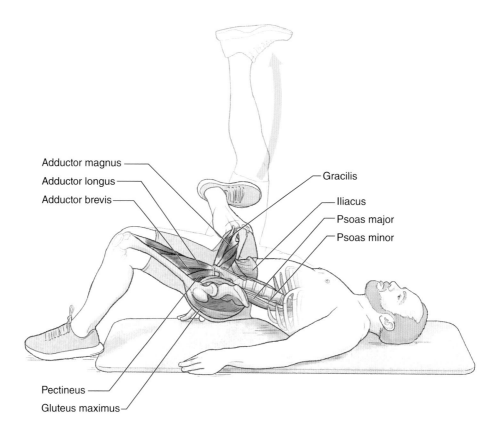

Adductor magnus

Adductor longus

Adductor brevis

Gracilis

Iliacus

Psoas major

Psoas minor

Pectineus

Gluteus maximus

Execution

1. Lie on your back and place your feet flat with your knees bent.
2. Lift one leg off the ground and straighten it toward the ceiling.
3. Raise the hips as high as possible, pushing off the planted leg, foot firmly on the ground.
4. Lower the lifted leg slowly to the side, keeping it in line laterally with the hips.
5. Just before the leg touches the ground, whip it back up to center.
6. Keep the hips high. Do not rotate the hips to the side the leg is falling toward.
7. Keep the whipping leg as straight as possible.
8. Perform for the allotted number of repetitions, and then switch to the other leg.

Muscles Involved

Primary: Adductor magnus, adductor longus, adductor brevis, pectineus, gracilis

Secondary: Gluteus maximus, psoas major, psoas minor, iliacus

HOCKEY FOCUS

The ability to recover in a skating stride is primarily achieved by engaging the adductors. Strong adductors enable you to pull the extended leg back under the body quickly and forcefully to then push off and propel into the next stride. The abductors and adductors should be balanced to prevent groin and lower-abdominal strains.

REACHING T-BALANCE CONE TOUCH

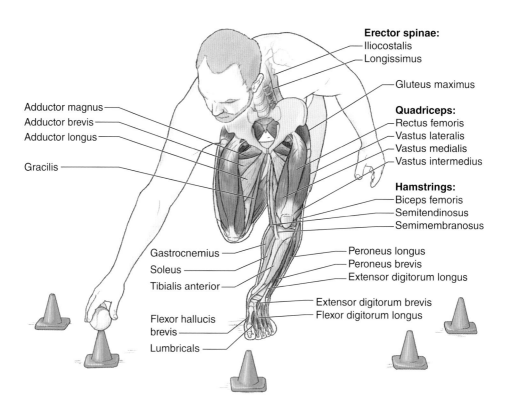

Erector spinae:
Iliocostalis
Longissimus

Gluteus maximus

Quadriceps:
Rectus femoris
Vastus lateralis
Vastus medialis
Vastus intermedius

Hamstrings:
Biceps femoris
Semitendinosus
Semimembranosus

Adductor magnus
Adductor brevis
Adductor longus

Gracilis

Gastrocnemius
Soleus
Tibialis anterior

Peroneus longus
Peroneus brevis
Extensor digitorum longus

Extensor digitorum brevis
Flexor digitorum longus

Flexor hallucis brevis
Lumbricals

Execution

1. Place three to five cones in a 180-degree arc.
2. With bare feet, stand in the middle of the arc on one foot.
3. Stand tall and reach the lifted foot behind you.
4. At the same time, lower the chest to form a T with the body.
5. Reach out to a cone and touch the cone or place a ball on top of it.
6. Stand upright, keeping the back foot off the ground.
7. Return to the T position and reach for another cone.
8. Repeat this pattern for the allotted number of rounds or place and pick up a ball at each cone.

Muscles Involved

Primary: Flexor digitorum longus, flexor digitorum brevis, flexor hallucis longus, flexor hallucis brevis, lumbricals, plantaris, extensor digitorum longus, extensor digitorum brevis, peroneus longus, peroneus brevis, hamstrings (semitendinosus, semimembranosus, biceps femoris), gluteus maximus, quadriceps (rectus femoris, vastus lateralis, vastus medialis, vastus intermedius)

Secondary: Erector spinae (iliocostalis, longissimus, spinalis), gastrocnemius, soleus, tibialis anterior, adductor longus, adductor brevis, adductor magnus, gracilis

HOCKEY FOCUS

The ability to balance while pivoting and moving on one leg is vital in hockey. The strength and stability of the ankle is important for prevention of injury. Also, this exercise elicits balance out of the skate that in turn leads to a more powerful initial push in skating or going from post to post for goalies.

VARIATION

Unstable Reaching T-Balance Cone Touch

To increase the balance challenge, perform the exercise on an unstable surface such as a balance pad or stability disc.

NECK NOD

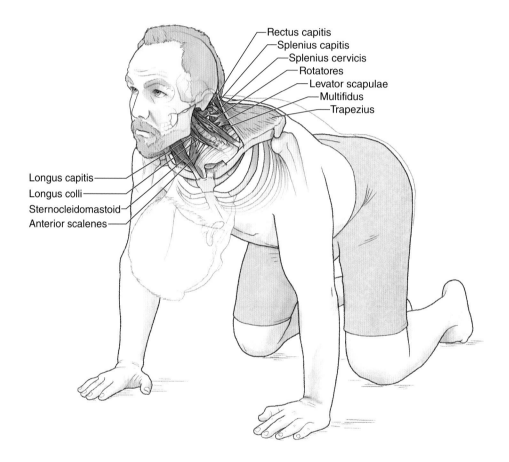

Rectus capitis
Splenius capitis
Splenius cervicis
Rotatores
Levator scapulae
Multifidus
Trapezius

Longus capitis
Longus colli
Sternocleidomastoid
Anterior scalenes

Execution

1. Assume an all-fours position on the ground.
2. Bring the chin to the chest as far as possible and hold that contraction for a three count.
3. Lift the head up and back while looking up as high as possible and hold that contraction for a three count.
4. Keep going back and forth slowly for the allotted number of repetitions, making sure all the movement comes from the neck.

Muscles Involved

Primary: Sternocleidomastoid, anterior scalenes, longus capitis, longus colli, levator scapulae, splenius capitis, splenius cervicis, rectus capitis

Secondary: Trapezius, multifidus, rotatores

HOCKEY FOCUS

A strong neck helps absorb impact to the head. Delivering or receiving a blow to the head can be stabilized through the strength of the neck. Strong neck muscles increase neck stability and can help prevent a whiplash effect during a blow to the head.

VARIATIONS

Isometric Neck Bridge With Exercise Ball

Stand facing a wall. Place an exercise ball, such as a Swiss ball, between your head and the wall. Walk the feet away from the wall so that the body is at an angle. Keep the head and ball pressed into the wall. Hold for the allotted time. Change position, performing the drill with both sides and the back of the head.

Neck Bridge on Bench

Lie on a flat weight bench with your head off the edge of it. Lie facing up to work the anterior neck muscles, facing down to work the posterior neck muscles, and on your side to work the opposite side lateral muscles. In a controlled motion, let the weight down slowly toward the ground. Then, using the neck, lift the weight towards the ceiling in a controlled motion. Hold a weight plate of 5 to 10 pounds (2-5 kg) on top of the head. Work the front, sides, and back of the head. Gradually increase resistance as strength increases. Make sure to use a light weight, if any, and to go slowly, making sure not to "jerk" the weight and the neck. The motion should be controlled and smooth, and only through the specific range of motion of the individual. It should not be a forced range of motion.

EXERCISE FINDER

SPEED

AGILITY

MOBILITY

BALANCE

CORE STABILITY

INJURY REHABILITATION

ABOUT THE AUTHORS

Michael Terry, MD, is the head team physician for the Chicago Blackhawks and a team physician for Northwestern University Athletics and the U.S. Olympic volleyball team. He is also the sports medicine program director and the Dr. Charles and Leslie Snorf Professor of Orthopcdic Surgery at Northwestern University.

Michael Terry

Terry graduated with honors from the University of Illinois with a degree in mechanical engineering and a concentration in bioengineering. He then attended the University of Chicago Pritzker School of Medicine, where he again graduated with honors and received the top honor in surgical specialties and in clinical medicine.

Terry completed a residency at Cornell University's prestigious Hospital for Special Surgery, where he was part of a team that was awarded one the most coveted research awards in shoulder surgery, the Neer Award. He then traveled to Vail, Colorado, for his sports medicine fellowship at the renowned Steadman Hawkins clinic.

Prior to joining the team at Northwestern, Terry was a faculty member at the University of Chicago. While there, he performed research and maintained a very busy practice in sports medicine and shoulder surgery. His medical school students selected Terry as their favorite faculty member.

Paul Goodman is the strength and conditioning coach for the Chicago Blackhawks and is responsible for preparing yearlong on- and off-ice training regimens for all players within the organization. He also works in conjunction with the sports medicine staff by assisting in the rehabilitation process for injured athletes.

© Human Kinetics

Goodman joined the Blackhawks after serving six years as head strength and conditioning coach at the University of Vermont (UVM). In 2006, the National Strength and Conditioning Association (NSCA) named Goodman the State/Provincial Director of the Year, and he also was a finalist for the NSCA's College

Strength and Conditioning Coach of the Year award. In addition to UVM, Goodman also spent time with USA Women's Hockey and the New York Rangers.

Goodman is a 1996 graduate of the University of Wisconsin, and he received his master's degree in 2002 while serving as a member of the Wisconsin Badgers' strength and conditioning staff. He achieved a second master's degree in applied exercise science from Concordia University of Chicago, where he is currently in pursuit of his PhD in health and human movement.